If a
Tree
Falls

OTHER BOOKS IN THE REUBEN/RIFKIN SERIES

Arguing with the Storm: Stories by Yiddish Women Writers
edited by Rhea Tregbov

Dearest Anne: A Tale of Impossible Love
by Judith Katzir

Dream Homes: From Cairo to Katrina, an Exile's Journey
by Joyce Zonana

Shalom India Housing Society
by Esther David

The Reuben/Rifkin Jewish Women Writers Series
A joint project of the Hadassah-Brandeis Institute
and the Feminist Press

Series editors: Elaine Reuben, Shulamit Reinharz, Gloria Jacobs

The Reuben/Rifkin Jewish Women Writers Series, established in 2006 by Elaine Reuben, honors her parents, Albert G. and Sara I. Reuben. It remembers her grandparents, Susie Green and Harry Reuben, Bessie Goldberg and David Rifkin, known to their parents by Yiddish names, and recalls family on several continents, many of whose names and particular stories are now lost. Literary works in this series, embodying and connecting varieties of Jewish experiences, will speak for them, as well, in the years to come.

Founded in 1997, the Hadassah-Brandeis Institute (HBI), whose generous grants also sponsor this series, develops fresh ways of thinking about Jews and gender worldwide by producing and promoting scholarly research and artistic projects. Brandeis professors Shulamit Reinharz and Sylvia Barack Fishman are the founding director and codirector, respectively, of HBI.

If a Tree Falls

A Family's Quest to Hear and Be Heard

JENNIFER ROSNER

THE FEMINIST PRESS
AT THE CITY UNIVERSITY OF NEW YORK
NEW YORK CITY

Published in 2010 by the Feminist Press
at the City University of New York
The Graduate Center
365 Fifth Avenue, Suite 5406
New York, NY 10016

feministpress.org

First printing, May 2010

Cover and text design by Drew Stevens

Library of Congress Cataloging-in-Publication Data

Rosner, Jennifer
If a tree falls : a family's quest to hear and be heard / by Jennifer Rosner.
    p. cm.
ISBN 978-1-55861-662-2
1. Deaf children. 2. Families. I. Title.
HV2391.R67 2010
362.4'20922—dc22
[B]

2010004198

PRINTED IN CANADA

For Bill,
Sophia, and Juliet

In this book I follow the convention whereby audiological deafness is spelled with a lowercase "d," to distinguish it from Deafness with an uppercase "D," a reference to the culture and community of those with fluency in sign language.

Prologue

FOR A LONG TIME, I thought this story began with my daughter's birth, or just a few hours later, when we learned that she might not hear. But the question of not hearing began long before her, before me.

A string, fragile and thin, a cilia strand, a helix, twists its way back in time to Brooklyn, New York, and before that, to tiny shtetls, specks on the maps of Eastern Europe. For generations, the line has been frayed and tattered.

But I am told that at one time, a cord gently linked our wrists so that we would wake together. Our hands clasped and our arms twined, thick as a seaman's rope.

And we could hear.
And we could listen.

California, July 2000

I WAS CALM WITH OUR NEWBORN BABY GIRL nestled in the crook of my arm. I hadn't expected to be calm in new motherhood. Yet, here I was with Sophia. Soaked and happy. Anchored by her gaze.

We had arrived at the hospital to find a nursing strike in full force. Our doctor, who'd assured us that he had no plans to travel in July, was away on vacation. We were settled into a labor room by a strikebreaker scanning the room for sterile gloves and fetal heart-rate monitors.

Bill got hold of a birthing ball and a cup of ice chips, and sought to soothe me with reminiscences of the day we conceived. It was Halloween morning and we had been trying to conceive for fourteen months. Bill proclaimed to me, with prophetic sureness: "YOU are getting pregnant today." We had a houseguest, but Bill just handed him the dog leash and a shopping list of assorted candy and ushered him out the door.

Now, nine months later, here was our girl, swaddled and warm, with wispy brown hair and huge slate eyes. Sophia.

Shoulder to shoulder with Bill in our narrow hospital bed, I lost myself in the chub of Sophia's feet and the translucent pink of her toenails as she dozed off to sleep. I hardly noticed the beeping monitors, the flurry and rush of nurses, the ring ring of the telephone. I was in a bubble, impervious to our surroundings. I had experienced this insulation only once before in my lifetime, when Bill and I stood together beneath our wedding chuppah, alight in a September's sunset six years earlier. My attention fixed only on him—his peacock blue eyes flickering in the candlelight, his sure voice, his vows, riding softly on the night air—until the shatter of glass brought forth the cheers of family and friends, Bill's lips to mine.

I was jarred out of our new magic when a hospital volunteer with a red and white polka-dotted hat wheeled in a computer cart and prepared to run the newborn hearing test. Unapologetically, she swabbed Sophia's forehead and applied electrodes in four places. Sophia stirred in sleep, but did not wake. Stepping gingerly around the computer wires, the volunteer came to stand at the keyboard, pushing keys and then waiting, staring at the monitor. Nurses had already been in and out for heel sticks, eye drops, immunizations, a vitamin K shot. I continued to gaze at Sophia.

She was all olive, rose, and brilliant slate gray, her features still mushy like a newborn pup's.

I glanced over at Bill to see if he noticed the way Sophia's lips pouted. I was surprised to find his face sallow. He was up, questioning the volunteer about the numbers that appeared on the screen. His stare alternated between Sophia and the computer monitor.

"What are the typical scores for this test?" Bill asked.

"The numbers are usually in the hundreds," the volunteer mumbled almost inaudibly.

I sat up and gaped at the tiny white numbers, dwarfed by the hulking black monitor: 4 . . . 7 . . . 3.

"Soph, you're not exactly setting the world on fire." Bill's voice was thin.

"Bill, what's going on?"

"*Come on*, Sophia."

The volunteer shifted her weight, staring at us awkwardly. Then she walked over to Sophia, removed the electrodes, and gently wiped the goo from Sophia's hairline. She stuffed the tangle of cords on a low tray, switched off the computer screen, and guided the computer cart, backward, out of the room.

An audiologist came in five minutes later. "I've been notified that Sophia didn't pass the hearing screen, but remember, your baby has been 'underwater' for nine months," she said in a reassuring voice. She went on to explain that residual amniotic fluid or a bacterial infection may have caused Sophia to fail the screening test. Statistics were in our favor: twenty-six of thirty babies who fail the initial test pass it two weeks later. Only a small number turn out to be hard of hearing or deaf.

I sat, silent, with Sophia curled in my lap.

The bright sunlight beamed through the thick hospital window. I had just finished my doctorate in philosophy, but lacked the philosophical tools to deal with this. My baby could be hard of hearing or deaf? How was this possible? Like all expectant mothers, I had harbored fears for my baby, choking down prenatal vitamins the size of horse pills and eating platefuls of kale to ward off the numerous maladies catalogued in the pregnancy books. But *deafness?* I'd had no reason to consider it. Now, despairing passages flashed through my head: Aristotle's notorious claim that the deaf, incapable of speech, are incapable of reason. Immanuel Kant's view that the "Dumb" (the mute) can never be full-fledged persons. The categorization, in Jewish law, of deaf mutes as forever childlike. I knew these conceptions were outdated, from another, less generous time, but they eroded my spirit anyway, and dreams I didn't realize I carried—dreams full of a child's chatter and song—began to wither deep inside.

The audiologist broke into my pained muddle with a pragmatism that was strangely comforting. "I can't have any idea what this must be like for you. I don't have a baby, never mind a baby that might be deaf." She went on to take down our history, asking if there was anyone with hearing problems in our families.

My mother. My mother had substantial hearing loss. She had worn hearing aids all of my life. They whistled and never seemed to work very well. But so far as I knew, my mother wasn't born with her hearing problem—she lost her hearing after a series of mastoid infections and surgeries. It wasn't genetic. I told the audiologist what I knew of my mother's history.

After the audiologist left, I dialed my parents in Connecticut. With Sophia in my lap, the phone cord bunched and tangled like curly hair just above her nearly bald head.

"Dad, Sophia failed the newborn hearing screening."

"What?"

"She didn't pass the hearing test. The audiologist said it might be due to fluid or a bacterial infection. They're going to test her again later. But . . ."

"Jenny, I'm sure it will clear up. Listen, we're flying out there in a few hours. We'll see you this afternoon."

"But what about mom's hearing loss? Is there any chance it's genetic?"

"No, no. Don't push the panic button. I'm sure it will all clear up."

Hours later, the same volunteer wheeled in the computer and re-tested Sophia. There again were those tiny white numbers—too low, much too low. Sophia lay asleep, unperturbed as Bill and I stood powerless: we couldn't will her to hear the sounds being piped into her brain.

My parents arrived in the early evening, gift bags filled with baby blankets and onesies rustling in their arms. They settled into our crowded hospital room and took turns cradling Sophia. The place teemed with people—nurses and doctors, lactation consultants, various friends wanting to meet Sophia, a "welcome wagon" lady from the local synagogue with a challah in tow. Through the clamor, I felt a burgeoning grief rise inside me. It clashed with my joy and wonder at Sophia—how she opened her tiny mouth like a baby bird, how she stretched all twenty-one inches of herself, from the tips of her fingers to the tips of her toes, as she yawned. Against my own groundless hopes, I recoiled from every attempt at reassurance. "She probably still has fluid in her ears," my parents kept saying. I could hardly look at Bill.

Later that night, my father walked to a nearby market to get us provisions: my favorite black currant tea, rice pudding, bagels and cream cheese, a pint of fresh blueberries.

Then my parents left. They would visit the next day, before their flight back. We were alone again. Bill and I nestled Sophia, capped and swaddled, into the bed. I stacked newborn diapers into the bureau drawer, ate a spoonful of rice pudding, then huddled next to Bill on the remaining swath of bed, burying my face in his shoulder. The prospect of middle-of-the-night feedings was a relief to me. I knew I wouldn't be sleeping tonight.

The following day, the audiologist came to schedule Sophia for further tests. She tried to reassure us again with statistics. I clutched the small, striped hospital blanket that Sophia was swaddled in at birth. Nurses bustled about, preparing us for discharge. We were handed a form to rate our comfort level with the various tasks of baby care: nursing, diapering, bathing. We were novices at all of it, unsure even of how to rate ourselves. I stood paralyzed beside the baby bassinet, wondering if it would be all right if we took the swaddle blanket with us. Our discharge papers contained the order to return to the hospital in two weeks for audiological follow-up.

Sophia's newborn diaper dangled off her tiny, silken body as I arranged her in her new infant car seat for the drive home. Upon our arrival, our German Shepherd, Lucca, barked out a welcome. I felt Sophia startle.

Inside, I settled Sophia in her crib, newly padded and

bumpered. Then I bustled about, preparing the nursery, and myself, for the continuous feeding and diapering cycles to come. With every sound—the closing of a drawer, the creak of a floorboard—my eyes darted to Sophia.

In the wee hours—our first night home with Sophia—I began to tie a string around the crib's maple post, like I had seen my grandmother do for good luck. As I looped the thin red cord into a flouncy bow, I heard the clicking and beeping of our fax machine. I entered my study to see pages falling in curls off the paper tray, brushing against my feet. I picked up the cover sheet, and in my father's distinctive, nearly illegible handwriting, read: *To Jenny, Love Dad*. I picked up the next page and saw that it was a family tree, scrawled in my father's hand. He must have added Sophia to it!

I gathered up the various pages and I saw that some of the names of my relatives were marked with an asterisk: Nellie*, Bayla*, Bertha*, Sam*, Moe*, Judith*. I wondered what the asterisks might mean. Could they connote relatives who died in the Holocaust? Other names on the chart had a tiny *OK* written next to them.

I rifled through the pages. At the very bottom of the last page:

* = *Deaf and Dumb*.

◆ ◆ ◆

My t-shirt dampened with cold sweat. I shivered. I couldn't seem to keep my hands, or the uncurled fax pages, steady. Sophia was crying—something I understood more from the cramping of my uterus and the letdown of my milk than from my sense of hearing.

I dialed my father—it was 7 a.m. in Connecticut. I could barely get any words out. He tried to dispel my worries. Again, he raised the audiologist's point that Sophia may have fluid in her ears or a bacterial infection—something that will resolve quickly. "But the audiologist hasn't seen our family chart," I sputtered bitterly. I knew my father wanted to protect me, but was he in utter denial?

When I showed Bill the chart, he hugged me tight.

"It's all right, Jenny. It's going to be all right."

"But how?" I countered. "There is deafness all around us."

There was my *mother's* hearing loss—which supposedly developed from infections in infancy, though now I couldn't help but wonder if it was actually a genetic, progressive hearing loss. And there was the documented deafness on my *father's* side of the family, too. Bill wasn't aware of any deafness in his family history. But we'd come to learn from a hasty Internet search that Ashkenazi Jews—Bill and

I were both of Ashkenazi descent—have a heightened risk of carrying recessive gene mutations for deafness. If Sophia had a hearing loss caused by recessive gene mutations, she'd have inherited one each from *both* of us.

For the next two weeks, I put Sophia down only to devise, run, and then discount homespun hearing tests. I'd settle her on the bed, stand behind her, and clap my hands; then I'd question whether the sudden gust of wind created by the clap could explain her eye blink as well as the clapping sound itself. Or I'd rig up a towel (to shield the wind gusts) only to watch my clapping coincide with the billowing out of a stray thread that tickled her thigh. Or I'd wrap myself with a thick blanket (to dull the scent of my breast milk) while I cut the frayed edges of the re-rigged towel (to prevent thigh tickling). Then I'd clap my hands and hear Lucca bark at the same moment, perhaps in protest to it all. Eventually, I'd take Sophia back into my arms, sink into the bed, and try to synchronize my breathing with her gentle, sleeping breaths.

◆ ◆ ◆

The morning of the follow-up appointment, Bill and I packed the diaper bag, settled Sophia into her car seat, and drove to the hospital. The jingle of bicycle bells. The ditty of an ice cream truck. A car honk from behind. We didn't speak. Bill looked ahead, driving. I stared out the window at the trees, a blur of gnarled greens and browns.

In a cramped testing room, we perched awkwardly on high stools and peered over the audiologist's shoulder at the computer monitor. Sophia lay asleep on a blanketed examination table, electrodes gooed to her head. Indecipherable sound waves, like peaking mountain ranges, appeared as sketches on the screen, then disappeared.

Nearly an hour passed before the audiologist turned off the computer and led us to a cluster of chairs in the corner of her office. Sophia woke with a start, her arms flailing, then fell back asleep on the table. A fluorescent light hummed overhead. The audiologist chose a huge yellow binder from the bookshelf, then came and sat across from us in a chair, the binder on her lap.

"Sophia has a severe sensorineural hearing loss," she began. She held up a page she had printed from her computer. It was a piece of graph paper spattered with little sound drawings: a barking dog, a ringing telephone, an airplane, a piano. There was a jumble of letters—the sounds of speech—clustered inside a banana-shaped outline. A sloping line, another mountain sketch, overlaid the drawings. The audiologist explained that the sloping line was Sophia's audiogram; it showed what range of frequencies and decibels Sophia could hear. Almost nothing in the "speech banana."

"So she can't hear us talk?" I asked hoarsely.

"No. She may hear some speech sounds—the wide open vowel sounds—but not much else."

The audiologist told us that the typical working ear has over fifteen thousand tiny hair cells that convert sound waves into neural signals. In Sophia's case, it was likely that a majority of these hair cells were broken or bent or missing. As she spoke, she handed me the binder. It was thick with information about deafness.

The audiologist enumerated possible causes of Sophia's hearing loss, beginning with recessive genes from Bill and me. I could see that I was shaking before I felt it. I darted to the examination table, scooped up Sophia, and rocked her back and forth, back and forth. She was so tiny, just two weeks old, her hands still transparent. *What would life be like for her? How were we going to communicate?* The audiologist spoke about hearing aids, about sign language, about the cultural divide between Deaf and Oral schools. She was saying that deafness was sometimes syndromic, and that tests would need to be ordered to rule out eye, kidney, and heart disorders. We should schedule a genetics consult, she added as she looked over my family chart. Bill came to stand next to me, and steadied my quaking hand.

♦♦♦

We drove home with the car windows up. I watched a cluster of businessmen standing together at a street corner, their faces animated with talk. One man's face contorted in laughter. Another's, in mock surprise. The car filled with Sophia's short, bleating cries, then quieted.

I racked my brain for memories, as I had each day since receiving the fax. Had anyone ever spoken of deaf relatives?

My sister knew the family history. She had told me last night over the phone.

"Yeah, I remember looking at the family tree. There were two deaf sisters—Dad's great-great aunts back in the 1870s. Some of their children and their children's children were deaf, too. Two of Dad's uncles—Sam and Moe. I don't know if he knew them."

I was shocked at what she knew. When did she learn all this?

My sister told me she wrote a paper on our family's geneology years ago, in high school. Grandma Rose had traced the family lines back to the Wertheim strand, and some cousins had worked on it too, on the Fleischer side. My sister had interviewed a few relatives who remembered Dad's uncles conversing in sign language at a family reunion. "I'm sure Dad assumed you knew this, too," my sister told me.

As a young girl, the youngest of four children, I was thrown in with the lot. At the dinner table, my older brothers were bursting with commentary, my sister, with earnest questioning. I couldn't get a word in. I tried raising my hand, hoping to be "called on" as if in school. I tried shouting. Often, it was a visiting relative, an aunt or an uncle, who would finally cut in. "Why are you yelling, Jenny?" "Because no one ever listens to me!" I was lost in the din.

Was I out of earshot when they spoke of deaf relatives? Or was I just not listening? There was deafness everywhere, up and down the limbs of my family tree! Not a word. Had I heard.

I slapped the thick binder against my legs. A break in the silence. Through the car window, the shade of loquat trees cast shadows across Sophia's face. Bill steered the car into our driveway.

I carried Sophia into the house and placed her in her crib. She was asleep, her hands fisted high above her head. "We'll fight together," I wanted to whisper in her ear.

I walked out of the nursery, swallowing.

California, August 2000

WITH SOPHIA, I LOST MY VOICE. Sophia couldn't hear it and I couldn't produce it. For weeks, I didn't talk, sing, or read aloud. I picked her up and held her tight.

Lucca sprawled herself out in a sunny spot beside the bed and licked her paw pads, each cracked line smoothed by the broad, wet slurp of her tongue. Why didn't her tongue get scratched or cut, I wondered, when her pads were edged sharp like cookie cutters? Lucca was licking her feet quicker and quicker, louder and louder. *Slap, lap; slap, lap; slap, lap.* I propped Sophia against my shoulder and clapped my hands together to make Lucca stop. Her chestnut eyes darted to me questioningly, her pointy ears wilting flat.

Bill was back at work, directing a nonprofit that advocated for abused and neglected children in dependency court. He oversaw the training and supervising of volunteers who met with the children, spoke to foster parents and teachers, and tried to determine best home placements. In court hearings, the "child advocates" made their recommendations to a judge.

When Bill arrived home each night—light- or heavy-hearted, depending on the judicial outcomes—he took care of us. He diapered Sophia and walked Lucca. He fetched me the nursing pillow, the swaddling blankets, the burping cloths. He hugged me as he did when we first met, his strength around me leaving me breathless. He cradled Sophia gently, his eyes crinkling into a loving smile, his lips puckering into a soft kiss.

When I expressed grief over Sophia's hearing loss, Bill brought a perspective he acquired from his work. His caseloads included a fifteen-year-old girl molested by three different relatives, a five-year-old boy starved in a house filled with food, an infant left alone for two days. Sophia was loved and cared for. She would thrive. Together, we'd see to it.

◆ ◆ ◆

When Sophia was awake, I tickled her cheeks and played "bicycle" gently with her legs. I bounced her up and down, and entertained her with finger puppets. Sophia's eyes widened with excitement when I brought my face close to hers from far away. Zoom. Kiss. Zoom. Kiss.

When she napped, I went to my desk and stared at the names on my family chart—those asterisked names—wondering about my deaf relatives. I worked my way through the audiologist's binder: I read about deafness and called the parents of deaf children willing to provide information and support. I pumped extra breast milk because Sophia's weight was low, and I prepared supplemental bottles. Friends came by with gifts, with food and hugs, and with the names of still other people to contact.

Bill and I were given the email addresses of two deaf grown-ups. Their childhood experiences were distressing. One woman described excruciating speech sessions in which she struggled to make vocalizations she could not hear—each utterance exchanged for a Froot Loop. At the age of sixteen, she became fluent in sign language and in the Deaf community found comfort and a sense of belonging for the first time in her life. The other wrote bitterly about how her parents sent her away to a Deaf school, largely severing their relationship with her. She felt she "belonged" at school but never at home. Since neither her parents nor her siblings learned Sign, holidays at home were endlessly lonely.

I had entered motherhood with my own pressing worries—worries that had nothing to do with a child's hearing loss; worries that came from my experience growing up amid intermittent connections and patchy hearing. Could I sustain a healthy connection with my baby? Could I mother my child whole? I felt full of holes, and the prospect of mothering disquieted me.

As a child, my mother's rapt gaze fed me, filled me up. When I had her affection—her huge seafoam eyes lavishly, generously, focused on me—I held the world in my outstretched hands. But I never had it for long. Distracted or in a rush, my mother would turn away from me. Tune me out. She was masterful at tuning me out. Her hearing loss played an incalculable role—she could slip into her own private reverie, block out the world, disengage from me instantly and entirely. When I reasserted myself, she was sharp-edged. Her gentle brushing of my hair became an impatient ripping of tangles. Her zippering of my dress, a jaw into my flesh. My protests, my cries only hastened her retreat.

What would I be like with Sophia? More than anything, I wanted to hear my baby. I wanted to be an anchoring force, steady and sure in my attention. As much as I worried about Sophia's hearing, I worried about my *own*. I didn't have a literal hearing loss, but I feared the disconnection I experienced in childhood. I feared it as if it was an inheritable trait.

♦ ♦ ♦

One morning while Sophia slept, I tried to nap but couldn't. I told myself I should shower, but instead I turned on the computer, and through the Internet entered the fractious and militant universe of deafness—the politics of inclusion and exclusion, the legacy of hurt feelings, the horror and awe of technological advancement.

There was a war going on. One side believed that deaf people should assimilate to the hearing culture by using hearing aids or cochlear implants to help them to hear and to speak. The other believed that deaf people should embrace Deaf culture, a world without sound, and communicate using sign language. The war was focused on new babies because deafness was now detectable at birth. Militants on the side of assimilation considered it a moral obligation to give babies access to the sounds of speech and access to the larger hearing world. Militants on the side of Deaf culture considered it a travesty to do so, arguing that deaf babies were being "altered" by technology, "mutilated" by surgeons, and stripped of their rightful membership in the Deaf community.

What side are you on? the websites taunted me. Would we try to get Sophia to hear with the latest hearing technology and then work on speech, on spoken language? Would we try to communicate with her in sign language?

I had stumbled into a minefield where any answer implied a prejudicial judgment. Was deafness a disability? Was it an essential identity? We wanted what was best for our baby, for our family! It was infuriating to think that our choices for Sophia were going to be judged by others, and on these terms.

I decided I'd better shower after all. Let the water wash over my thoughts.

In the shower's mist, a shaft of bright light cast a prism rainbow on the white tile wall. I closed my eyes tight and bent my head into the spray. In another time and place, we wouldn't have had these decisions to make for our deaf child. Pearl—the mother of the deaf sisters, Nellie and Bayla, listed on my family chart; she raised her babies in a remote Austrian shtetl with neither the luck nor the burden of modern options, with no choices concerning technology or education. What could she do but tote them along with her to the baker, to the butcher, to the synagogue, to the town square? And wonder what it was like for her girls, to weave in and out of the rickety stalls among the mingled smells of horse dung and hay; to watch the swirl of changing expressions—the winking eyes, the pursed lips, the bushy beards—but *never to hear* the sounds of the bargaining, the beckoning, the greeting, the gossiping, blurted and sputtered and whispered and hissed.

Was that Sophia crying? I rushed out of the bathroom, grabbing a towel, and I stood dripping in front of my baby. Her eyes were fixed on the slats of sunlight crossing through the bars of her crib. I touched her cheek. She turned to look at me. Droplets of water ran from my hair and splashed soundlessly onto the wood floor.

California, September 2000

WHEN SOPHIA WAS SIX WEEKS OLD, we ventured a cross-country flight to visit my parents and other family and friends. Early on a Friday morning, I lugged a last, over-stuffed suitcase to the driveway while Bill loaded the car for the airport. Then, I folded my father's fax sheets into my carry-on handbag, along with two tiny yellow mittens to keep Sophia from scratching herself while she slept. My hands shook as I zippered the bag. I was frayed from the middle of the night feedings. And I was preoccupied, consumed with trying to understand my family history, my deaf origins.

Day and night, my mind restlessly conjured images. From mere names on the genealogical page arose ashen cheeks, searching eyes, stubborn hands—whole lives fated to be filled with losses I shuddered against, even as I invented them. I scrutinized the pages of my family chart like a treasure map, like tea leaves, like the palm of a hand.

What heritage had I passed on, without knowing, to my baby?

I buckled Sophia into the car and pulled myself in to sit beside her. Soon I would learn whatever it was that I had missed of the family history. I would ask my parents every question I could think of, and call every living relative who might know something about our family's deafness. I would talk to my two brothers and to my sister. We each had different childhood memories.

In my parents' too-hot kitchen, decorated "country French," I inhaled the familiar smells of perfume, pipe tobacco, and chicken sautéing in wine. I greeted my mother and father tenderly as they surrounded us, hugging us and cooing over Sophia. My love for them, and my longing to be babied in new motherhood, mingled with trepidation. I was off-kilter in my parents' rambling house, even with Bill by my side and Sophia anchored in my arms.

That afternoon, I stood before the mirror in my mother's bathroom, cradling Sophia. My mother came to stand behind me. Her lips were glossed the color of raspberries and her salon blonde hair was styled in high coiffure. She looked at her granddaughter, then at her own reflection.

"She is absolutely beautiful. Don't worry about the hearing loss—with those eyes, she'll be just fine."

"What?"

"Where do you think she got those eyes?" her stare darting between the reflection of Sophia's eyes and her own.

"From Bill," I said.

"You think?" My mother's smile wavered.

Just then, I heard my father playing the violin. He had played every day of my life. The sound grew louder. A section of a Bach violin sonata, then a simple scale. I opened the bathroom door to see my father there in the hallway. He walked toward us, his chin still cocked on the rest, his right arm making long, broad strokes with his bow. The violin quivered within inches of Sophia's ear, flecks of rosin dusting her cheek. Sophia didn't turn to the sound.

"No, nothing," my father muttered. His bow hand dropped to his side.

So there it was: the proof of Sophia's hearing loss. It had come, not through last month's brainstem tests or audiograms, but through the unheard Cs and B flats of my father's violin.

◆ ◆ ◆

As a girl, I took up the violin. And I dressed myself like my mother. I teetered in her spike high heels, and painted my face with her glossy makeup. I even flapped in her silk blouses and whooshed leg-to-leg in her funny leather pants. Decked out in her clothes, adorned in her gold, I sang to her.

At age eight, I sang whatever I learned in school. By eleven, I had amassed a repertoire of Broadway show tunes. My mother made requests: "Everything Was Beautiful at the Ballet" from *A Chorus Line*; "Not While I'm Around," from *Sweeney Todd*; "Far From the Home I Love," from *Fiddler on the Roof*; "And I'm Telling You I'm Not Going," *from Dreamgirls*. I trailed after her, from her dressing room to the bathroom mirror, and sang to her as she got dressed to the nines.

Would she ever have guessed that I liked her best at nighttime when she was in her robe, no makeup on? Her eyes were a shade paler somehow, her face softer than when powdered and tawny, her lips sweeter when no longer waxy and bright. Even at a young age, I intuited that the slathered-on foundations, the layering of brilliant colors, were compensation for ears that couldn't hear well, for a father who didn't stay, for a mother who couldn't cope.

My mother blasted through many barriers of the times. She was determined to be self-sufficient. She earned her social work doctorate and launched a career. But her focus was on appearances—her own appearance and those of her extensions: our house, my brothers and sister, me. She loved me fiercely, and I loved her. Only I couldn't fix her attention on my being.

I made her things: a mop doll, a woodland diorama in a bowl. She thanked me tightly, then set about dismantling my handiwork—washing out the mop, dumping the twigs from the bowl, putting the house to rights—before she scurried off, retreating once more to her dressing room. I sat and watched her then from the periphery, a smudge at the edge of her looking glass.

I waited for her. I spent hours waiting. She chose a camisole from her closet. She styled her hair. My chatter, my questions, even my songs—nothing could retrieve her. She was distracted, lost in her own thoughts. I called out for her, still waiting. Couldn't my mother hear me?

◆ ◆ ◆

Edging my way out of my mother's bathroom, I gently swayed Sophia back and forth in the cradle of my arms. All I wanted was to wrap myself around and around my baby. Protect her. Reflect her. I positioned her in the baby carrier, facing in and snuggled close, and I squeezed by my parents. My mother was still in front of her mirror. My father watched me from the doorway, his violin extending downward from beneath his cocked chin.

In the kitchen, I settled myself into an armchair with raisin toast and tea. The dining table was already set for Shabbat dinner. While Sophia napped, I called as many relatives as I could, probing their memories. I worked my way through my parents' Rolodex, inquiring about our deaf ancestors. Relative after relative, their voices shaky and old, strained with earnest effort, then wilted with regret over lost recollections. Uncle Franklin and Aunt Shirley, on one family branch. Uncle Bob and Aunt Etti, on another.

Eventually, I reached my father's cousin, Phyllis, in Colorado. Phyllis's voice was authoritative, if crackly. She had a clear memory of my father's deaf uncles, Sam and Moe. She was insistent that they were deafened in childhood, not genetically, but as a result of the 1918 flu. So much family deafness, yet none of it claimed as genetic. I could practically see the lines of DNA crouched in hiding, dodging responsibility.

Phyllis remembered watching Sam and Moe sign together in their apartment in the Bronx. They had a light over their kitchen table that blinked when someone rang the doorbell. On the family chart, they were listed as Pearl's grandsons, asterisks near each of their names. Both men married deaf women. Sam and his wife had a deaf daughter, Judith Fleischer.

"Judy may still be alive; she'd be around your father's age," Phyllis offered.

If only I could find *her*—the one deaf relative who might connect me to all the others! My father's fax had catapulted me into the past, past the isolation I felt amidst my family into a search for long-ago connections. I wanted to learn all I could about my deaf ancestors. Were they happy? Were they heard? Were they integral to the life of their family, or did they stare on from the periphery, as if through a pane of glass? My deaf cousin might know something.

Phyllis told me she was in touch with a few relatives who might know of Judith's whereabouts. She would try and locate her.

◆ ◆ ◆

I flipped through the Rolodex and dialed another number. Sophia woke and nestled against me. As I spoke again—this time to an aunt in Florida—Sophia burrowed her face under my neck. Could she feel me talking? I tightened the straps of the baby carrier, hoisting her closer.

After the call, which yielded nothing, I put Sophia down on a knitted blanket. I held her hand against the bottom of a small tom tom drum while I tapped its taut center. Sophia's short legs kicked wildly. Tap tap. Another round of kicks.

I put Sophia's palm to my throat, and haltingly, I sang my first lullaby to her. Choked it out, knowing she couldn't hear it. My voice was classically trained and strong—I had studied since the age of thirteen with a former singer of the Metropolitan Opera—yet all that I could muster now was a breaking melody. "Brahms' Lullaby," hoarse and thin.

Bill rubbed the small of my back, kissed me on the cheek. Then he took out the furry, fuzzy, rubbery, bumpy toys we had stuffed into our suitcase. He tickled Sophia with a small purple feather and she squealed with delight. I cleared my throat, then grabbed a lemon from the kitchen counter and put it to her nose. Sophia opened her eyes wide.

Bill and I were up through the night for feedings and diapering. I felt grateful that Lucca, at least, was spared the wake-ups these few nights while we were traveling. Ever since we brought Sophia home from the hospital, Lucca woke to guard me while I nursed Sophia. In the wee hours, night after night, she'd hoist herself up, plod from our bedroom to the nursery, and drop down at the foot of my rocker with a deep-throated rumble. Her ears would remain pricked, attentive to my every rustle. Lying on the front porch beside the dog-sitter as we drove off to the airport, Lucca's face was furrowed with exhaustion.

Early the next morning, I made another call while Bill strolled Sophia along a woodsy path. If Bill was tiring of my ancestry obsession, he was indulgent enough not to show it. I dialed Blossom, my mother's cousin. I doubted that she could shed light on the origins of my mother's hearing loss. And the documented deafness was on my father's side. But I was taking a broader view of my family's hearing issues—the intermittent attentions, the flickering perceptions, the deafness that encompassed more than damage of the ears.

Blossom had a trove of stories about my mother's side of the family. She told me that my grandmother, Mae, was raised by two aunts on a farm in Poland after her mother died in childbirth and her father fled the scene. As a young girl my grandmother traveled to America and married my grandfather—also the progeny of a fugitive—who became impatient and restless after my mother was born and one day drove off, taking with him my mother's little girl heart.

Blossom described my mother as a child, her beginnings with her brother in a small Mount Vernon apartment filled with glazed porcelain roosters—brown wings, red chests, yellow beaks, and black clawed feet. As she spoke, I wondered at how such fragile things could populate a house so ravaged by brokenness. I knew that my mother had a difficult childhood, one marked by her parents' break up, by her hearing loss, and later, by a need to starve herself. I knew that my mother was ten when her father drove away for the first time, leaving her mother forlorn among fake roosters, struggling to rescue her pride. I used to touch those roosters—run my finger along their plumed wings, bent claws, glassy eyes—as I stood in my grandmother's crowded apartment amidst the scent of mothballs and hairnets. Back then I hadn't known how my grandmother had scrubbed herself clean after the long boat ride from Poland, changing in the Macy's bathroom before tracking down her runaway father in Brooklyn and venturing to his flat; how she watched as disappointment—or was it disgust?—flickered across her father's bearded face as he stood gaping at her from his threshold; how she came to recognize the look of flight in her new husband's eyes; how my mother came to look for it in everyone's eyes. A glint at first, a slight turn inward, perhaps. Then away. An absence, pulsing through the generations, chasing away presence.

Later in the day, I asked my mother if she would tell me about her past, about her family. "I have a dazzling picture of my parents," she said. "Wait 'til you see it." My mother rushed down the hall, her heels clicking along the terra cotta floor, her hearing aids whistling with feedback. She returned with an old photograph in a gilded frame, her face triumphant. Her parents were pictured in the bloom of their romance, peeking out of their 1930s car. Her father wore his hat brimmed rakishly above his almond eyes; her mother smiled shyly, adorned in white pearls.

As I stared at the photograph, I remembered the feel of my mother's necklaces, thin gold strands in a bumpy, jumbled mound. When I was a child I spent hours cross-legged on her bedroom floor, working out the knots. My mother always asked me to untangle them because I was patient and painstaking. When I brought her the unknotted necklaces, shimmering in long loops, her eyes gleamed and she smiled widely. Later, in a rush, she would try the necklaces on, reject them one by one, none quite right, and throw them hastily in a twisted pile.

"Do you know why he ran off?" I asked, looking at the image of a grandfather I had never met, debonair in black and white. "Did he ever return, did he try to make contact with you? Did he even know about your hearing problems?"

"Oh, Jenny, I don't want to talk about all *that*."

◆ ◆ ◆

I set aside my family research for the time being. We had only a few days left on the east coast, and we hadn't yet introduced Sophia to nearby friends and relatives.

On the last night of our visit, I found my father down-stairs in his study, the cool basement air thick with the smell of pipe tobacco. I asked him to tell me what he knew of our deaf relatives, the ones with the asterisks on his family tree.

My father told me that his grandmother, Sarah, was one of eight children in the Wertheim family. The deaf girls, Nellie and Bayla, were her sisters. He'd learned from his mother that Nellie and Bayla were tutored to become literate and that Bayla was further educated at a school for the deaf. Nellie and another sister, Elish, married two brothers from the same family, both printers by trade.

I wondered if those brothers were deaf, too. There were no marks by their names on the family tree, but from the reading I'd done, printing was a likely profession for the deaf because it was solitary and the noise of the working press wasn't a bother to them.

Why didn't my father ever talk about all this? Why didn't he say something when Sophia failed the hearing test?

My father's brown eyes peered at me over the thick horn rim of his eyeglasses. "Jenny, your mother and I found out all we could about the family's deafness before having you children. We brought the family chart to a geneticist. We were told that the family branches with deaf relatives on them were too distant from ours to indicate a genetic transfer. That's why I didn't mention it to you when you called from the hospital." My father unrolled his leather tobacco pouch, packed his pipe and lit it. I stood, looking at him. His hair was peppered gray. His eyes were cloudy, soft. I clutched the white painted banister.

"There's one other detail, Jenny," my father's voice was slightly hoarse. "It's always stayed with me. Tante Nellie and Tante Bayla—they tied strings from their wrists to their babies at bedtime. When the babies fidgeted, they would feel their tugs and wake to care for them in the night."

Strings, wrist to wrist: ties in the darkness to combat disconnection! I reeled with this image, this innovation of hearing. I stepped toward my father and bent slightly. He kissed me on the top of my head, like a small child.

California, October 2000

HOME IN CALIFORNIA, with my toes nestled beneath Lucca's soft fur as she lay at my feet, I scanned websites, studied American Sign Language hand forms, and read what I could about deafness. Every fact, every anecdote cast new shadows in my mind, bouncing into my fears, my hopes, for Sophia. I figured out how to nurse Sophia, even change her diaper, while using the phone, dialing still more relatives rumored to have worked on our shared family tree. I didn't leave the house much. It felt like a relief, one Friday evening, to dress myself and Sophia in fancy clothes and drive to a party at Bill's office.

Cradling Sophia in my arms while clutching the Styrofoam edge of a cup between my fingers, I weaved my way around the crowded reception room. Bill was mingling, beaming with pride as people rushed and fawned over Sophia. I sipped my iced tea.

Bill explained to some coworkers that we were considering high-powered hearing aids for Sophia. The audiologist thought they might give Sophia usable access to spoken language. She could be fitted for them within a month. Bill's manner was upbeat, undaunted. I still spent my days and nights tripping over piles of loss and worry, but Bill leapt right over these.

"Why don't you let her be who she is?" The man standing to my left was admiring Sophia and speaking to me.

"What?" I asked.

"Why don't you let Sophia be who she is?"

"Who *is* she?" I looked at Sophia. She was two months old. Did she have an identity yet?

"She is deaf," he answered. "She was born without access to sound. Why not let her live that way?"

Deaf. That couldn't be *who Sophia is*, could it? Just as I started to object, he excused himself to chase a tray of stuffed mushrooms.

Was it one hundred degrees in here? I gulped my iced tea and scanned the crowded room, noticing for the first time how low the ceiling was. I switched Sophia to my shoulder and peeled off my sweater. I didn't want to mingle. I didn't want a curried chicken skewer. What I wanted was to be connected with my baby.

I felt my face flushing. My Styrofoam cup didn't transfer any cold to my cheek.

◆ ◆ ◆

At home, later that night, I walked into the nursery to check on Sophia. She was swaddled cozily in her lavender striped pajama suit, sleeping soundly. But Bill was hunched over her crib, his face buried in his arms. His body was heaving, inches above the crib railing. I touched his shoulder.

Bill wiped his wet face with his sleeve. His puffy, tear-filled eyes met mine. "I guess I just lost it," he said. I hugged him tight. "Or maybe I found it." He laughed through his sniffles. "I don't know."

◆ ◆ ◆

That night, I was unable to sleep. I couldn't stop thinking about Bill. About Sophia. About my great-great aunts Nellie and Bayla, tying a string from their wrists to their babies in the night. A line, an anchor, a way of hearing their children. I had to find out *more*: how they fared, what became of them. Did anyone before make an effort to know them? I stole into my study and turned on the computer. I could try an ancestry search.

Within minutes, I was staring at a 1910 Census Report that showed Nellie Wertheim living in Brooklyn, New York! Born in 1871, to Pearl and Moshe Wertheim, her occupation was listed as sewing corsets. She emigrated from Austro-Hungary, the Gallizien Province.

Had Nellie's sister, Bayla, emigrated with her? I searched for Bayla Wertheim in all available US Census Reports. No records. I searched for their mother, Pearl. Nothing. Pearl's other six children. No.

What about Judith Fleischer? My cousin Phyllis had not yet located her. Upon typing in her name, the computer screen filled with listings. The Fleischer name was more common than I'd supposed. Without a birth date or home address, I'd never find her. I narrowed my search using her parent's names, Sam and Gertrude Fleischer. No matches.

I was restless. I longed to know my ancestors' *stories*—especially Pearl's and her children's. But how would I ever uncover them? I couldn't glean Nellie's experience from a single Census Report. In the shtetl books I'd read, the portrayals of deaf people were heartbreaking. The deaf were considered mentally impaired, isolated, and ostracized. *Is that how my ancestors lived?*

For the first time, I felt part of a larger line, reaching back to the past and stretching forward into the future. With the faxed pages of my family tree scattered around me, I opened a new blank journal I'd bought. It was bound in soft black leather, with a long string meant to mark a last writing page then wrap round and round to keep the journal closed. From down the hall, I could hear Sophia rustling in sleep, Bill snoring softly. I stared at the curves and dips in the stucco walls of my study. I breathed in the pulpy scent of the blank page, open before me.

For the moment, I was left with just my own imagining.

Galicia, 1871

WHEN YOU FIRST TRY TO LISTEN, *all you hear is noise. So much noise.*

In the shtetl, the noise of men is the din of argument. A challenge to interpretation. A reconstruction of theory. In a circle, rounded with pride, shrouded in humility, trumped up with faith, the men pester their texts, tease their minds, and block out the cries of their own and everyone else's hearts. The noise of women is the ruffle of contempt for the men who pester texts, the cackle of gossip and the grind of work and the hardening of hearts that chokes a child's whinny.

The cloudy morning of 17 Adar, in the Hebrew year 5630, a baby's wails rip through the Gallizien village of Tasse. Just two days old and little Shimon, Pearl and Moshe's boy, is filled with inconsolable sorrow. Boiling but ashiver, wriggling and swollen red. Pearl bounces and bobs him. She rocks him, rubs him, wraps him to her chest in her scarf of azure.

Pearl's mother hovers about with damp cloths, her eyes settling deep in their sockets. Pearl's father, with his left arm wound in leather straps, fastens a fragment of scripture to his head. Then he ushers Moshe out of the house, away from the women, off to shul.

Before going, he ties a string around the baby's hot ankle, and as they walk down the narrow village streets of Tasse, he lets the spool out. The thin cord—twined with hay along the side of Malkie's barn, muddied in a puddle along the river path, pulled taut by a snag in the stake of Golde's herb stand—trails its way to the synagogue's wooden Ark. Three times, Pearl's father coils the string around the thick scrolled posts, making a graceful swag in front of the gold brocade curtain that conceals the Torah. Moshe drops to his knees, breathes in the cool stone and must of the shul, and beseeches God—blessed be He—to hear their prayers for the baby.

Shimon's wails stop late that afternoon. He is buried the next day. Pearl sits on the earthen floor, her womb still in cramps, her breasts aching, full, as tears drain from her eyes. Moshe sits beside her, his shirt collar ripped in mourning. For seven days, sitting, Moshe hardly looks at Pearl. His unfocused eyes are glazed over with the wash of death.

◆ ◆ ◆

Pearl fights to remember how Moshe's eyes looked before Shimon. She hasn't known him so very long; their marriage was arranged with a short engagement, the baby conceived quickly. They were just finding their place together, cramped in her parents' house, establishing sweet rituals, new intimacies— her gentle fingers upon his thought-worn temples; a surprise of sweet, sliced apricots at her bedside table. A month after the burial, Moshe barely looks at her.

But now he takes Pearl's hand. It is Friday night, and her parents are still at the table, sipping hot tea through sugar cubes between their teeth. Moshe leads Pearl to his bed. He undresses her, slowly.

Moshe's eyes linger upon Pearl, not lustfully, but stubbornly, as if in a challenge to retrieve himself. His sunken jaw causes Pearl's own sorrow to flare. Every one of her nerves twitches, firing to get up, to run. But she lies nearly still. Her eyes drop to appraise her belly, still slack from childbirth. Moshe lifts himself onto her, enters. Pearl does not so much as touch his shoulder. She stares at the ceiling, at a crack in the plaster wall. With each push, she tightens.

Is he trying to hurt her? Is this how it is going to be—has she lost them both? Finally, Pearl rolls, toppling Moshe to his side, wet and cold outside of her. Moshe takes hold of a clump of Pearl's hair. He winds it around his bent forefinger and brings it to his lips. Sniffling, he clutches onto her, and together they fall, hollow, into sleep.

◆ ◆ ◆

Who knows how you find your steps after losing your footing? Life grinds on, and your feet teach you how to walk along. Pearl is pregnant again. Fear and hope clot, then thin her blood. Her mother spits left and right to keep trouble at bay. Moshe coils himself around Pearl's growing figure, cradling her in the night.

The night before she goes into labor, Pearl wakes to the pops and crackles of shattering glass. The smell of burnt straw. Bands of drunken peasants are running through the shtetl streets with flaming torches and rocks, screaming and breaking the windows of every Jewish shop and home. Pearl's father hurtles into Pearl's bedroom, grabs her by the arm, and shimmies her into the back hallway.

At dawn's light, while the men sweep shards of glass from the streets, a horde of women crowd into Pearl's house. They rub her back, try to lessen the pain shooting down her legs. Pearl can't help thinking about the tomorrow of her first labor—Shimon's quivery form. Her womb cramps tight as if to hold the baby in. The women eye each other sideways, while headlong they blurt assurances.

Pearl hasn't slept all night because of the peasant attack. Perhaps a rest will help. She lies down for a minute—until the pain propels her up again. A little walk, a tight circle in the cramped room; a waft of light, a look out the window. Then her legs are spread, her belly wrenching in upon herself, her ears a-ring with shouting. "A head, I see a head!" "How much hair already!" Another breath, a searing rip, and finally the baby is out. A girl. Another chance. A robust cry to ring in the smoke-choked dawn.

California, October 2000

IN THE MORNING, I HUDDLED in bed with Sophia draped on top of me. I stroked her soft hair, her warm cheek. Why had I imagined Pearl losing her first child? There was no baby—no Shimon—listed as deceased on my family chart. Of the eight children listed, I knew only that Pearl's daughters, Nellie and Bayla, were deaf. Whatever I grieved—Sophia's hearing, the loss of an ideal for my baby—this imagined death *far* outstripped it. I fetched my journal, splayed open on the study desk. With the long leather string I tied it shut, then shoved it deep into my dresser drawer.

After breakfast Bill and I walked tentatively, hand in hand, through the park. Sophia was burrowed close to me in the baby carrier, asleep. It was Saturday, and a cool breeze sent the leaves to billowing. The flyer had said that the Deaf playgroup would convene at picnic table 15A. As we approached the area, we saw parents and children soundlessly greeting each other, conversing with fast, crisp hand movements and animated facial expressions. A woman caught sight of me and made an admiring face as she looked upon Sophia, nearly hidden by her floppy hat. I nodded politely, even as I felt my body pull inward. I had to remind myself to breathe. It was quiet all around me except for the occasional tapping sound of hand against hand, or a faint, involuntary vocalization.

Bill and I had taken our first sign language class the week before—an evening class at a nearby community college. The room was filled with twenty-somethings in search of a fun elective. We wheeled in Sophia, asleep in her stroller. Bill said he would take her outside if she woke. Exhausted but desperate to learn, we fumbled awkwardly in an attempt to copy the movements and expressions of the teacher and the students all around us. We watched their hands, free to soar, as ours clenched with necessity and grief.

Now, milling around the picnic table, our smiles were forced, our movements awkward. We could do little more than wave and introduce ourselves by laboriously finger-spelling our names. Deaf parents conversed easily with one another as children scampered off toward play structures and swingsets. My mind flooded with anxieties: How would we ever gain fluency in this language? If hearing aids didn't work for Sophia, would we need a live-in interpreter, a third person, to help us talk to our daughter?

We walked beyond the picnic area, then found a narrow path leading to a river. Downhill from us, a little boy, no older than three, began running down the bank. His father rushed after him, waving his arms wildly, the biggest motions his body could make, signing to his son to stop. The boy did not see his father's motions. His eyes were fixed on the glittering water and the white bloom of mountain laurel as he moved headlong, closer and closer. I gasped and shouted out senselessly to the boy. Bill began to sprint, then slowed as the father loped to his son. In time. Just in time to keep him from tumbling into the river.

On the car ride home, Sophia woke up. Her big round eyes, glassy from sleep, now made me think of my mother's eyes, huge marbles the color of the sea. As a child, they were to me an inlet to an incalculable tide. Sometimes they lapped me up and rocked me in their sweet, frothy wake. Other times they swept past me, as I bobbed unsteadily, alone. I used to sit, legs dangling, on my mother's tiled bathroom counter as she made up her face in the gilded mirror.

"Mom?"

No answer.

"Mom?"

No answer.

"Mom!"

"What, honey?"

"Mom, what color is the sky?"

"Yup."

Was it her hearing loss? Or her need to tune out? To escape? Was it sheer exhaustion, raising four children and tracking conversations through the muddle of amplification? Why didn't anyone help my mother when she was a child—get her hearing aids, teach her speech reading—support her so she could listen, so she could hear?

As Bill drove the car, I stated what I wanted:

I wanted Sophia to be safe.

I wanted her to hear.

I wanted to hear her.

I wanted to be heard.

California, November 2000

DAY AND NIGHT, I STUDIED Sophia's searching eyes, her pouty lips, her tiny hands. Her fingers were long and delicate, her nails translucent pink. Maybe she could learn to talk, to have whole conversations, with those hands. But would we ever be able to understand her? Could we master enough sign language to truly communicate, to share complicated feelings, discuss complex ideas? I feared our interactions would be over-simplified and artificial. I feared we wouldn't be close or connected if I was fumbling to communicate in a second language. It could be Greek or Mandarin or Arabic. I wasn't adept.

I struggled each day to practice and learn Sign, but it came too slowly. I now had a stack of instruction books, index cards, a dictionary, a CD-ROM. I was inspired by the beauty of the language—the sensuality, the sense of it. I labored to build up a small vocabulary, but then I found myself forgetting signs, or mixing signs up. The sign for "summer" is similar to the sign for "black" and to the sign for "because." And these are all difficult to distinguish—if you lack the proper flourishes—from "don't know" and "forget." In the midst of new motherhood, I couldn't imagine forging my relationship with Sophia in this foreign language.

I tried to envision Sophia's future as a toddler, a teenager, an adult. Things we took for granted—whispering in a friend's ear, talking on the telephone—how could these things be closed off for her? Would her opportunities for friendship, for love, for work, be limited if she were never to hear or speak? On her blue and pink flecked baby blanket, Sophia batted her arms like an orchestra conductor, as if marking out a concerto's time with an invisible baton. I scooped her up and held her. Just held her and breathed her in. And breathed her out. And breathed her in again.

Everywhere we went, my own ears burned with what she missed—a snippet of Mozart through a neighbor's window, the tap-tap of a woodpecker on the forest path, the soft trickle of water at the stream. On our walks, I shifted Sophia from the stroller to the baby carrier so that she could feel the vibrations of my voice. Then I'd force myself to speak about the scene around us. "See that bird? That's a robin. Robins eat worms. And they sing, Sophia. They sing beautiful bird songs." A lump would rise, then, and choke my throat, and I'd struggle against it, worrying that Sophia could feel the vibrations of my sorrow as I swallowed.

I'd be silent, after that, and my mind would occupy itself with fighting philosophers. Kant's view that Deaf-Mutes could never attain concepts: it was wrong, premised on the false belief that the signs the Deaf use are incapable of universality. Modern linguists recognize Sign as a complete, natural language, not just a system of mere gestures . . .

In the midst of my internal rants, I'd look down at Sophia, and see her huge seal-pup eyes locked on me. My hopes for Sophia always buoyed when I caught her watching me. She stared at my face, especially at my mouth, with intensity. I'd start up again, speaking to her, pointing out the redwood trees, the streams, the striated rocks. Maybe she was hearing me when I spoke, at least partially?

I thought of Pearl as I walked on. Did she think that her deaf daughters could hear her at first? I'd had so little time with Sophia before the news of her hearing loss. Just hours before that hatted lady strode into our hospital room with that cart. How I'd wished for a full day, a week, a month with my baby, unworried by the news. It seemed a curse and a blessing now, to be beset by research and tests and findings. In Pearl's day, before there was hearing technology, it probably didn't matter that deafness could be more or less severe. Now, there were brainstem tests and audiograms documenting the precise degrees and contours of hearing loss. There were hearing aids and cochlear implants, signing schools, and manual schools. A myriad of options that at once heartened and disheartened us.

Our options for communicating with Sophia included signing, speaking, or some combination of signing and speaking, together. The pros and cons of each tugged at us and tied us in knots.

In theory, sign language would provide Sophia with language access right away, without risk of conceptual delays. At three months old, Sophia was already moving her fingers in imitation of my signing efforts. But the prospect of our becoming fluent was overwhelming. We couldn't possibly express ourselves fully in Sign—at least, not anytime soon. For Sophia to gain full exposure to sign language, we'd have to hire a translator, an interpreter, someone in between us and our baby. We felt our intimacy with Sophia threatened. Possibly even more troubling was the fact that her options in the larger world as a signing Deaf person would be pointedly constrained; only .02 percent of people in the United States were fluent in sign language. How could we keep her from growing up isolated, or marginalized?

Our audiologist put us in touch with a mother who combined Sign with speaking—the Total Communication approach—to communicate with her deaf three year old. When we met up with her family at an outdoor market, we saw that her child was almost exclusively signing his responses. As we talked to audiologists, speech pathologists, and teachers of the deaf, we came to believe that, in most total communication settings, signing took over as the predominant modality. Because speaking proved far more challenging for deaf children, Sign became the default.

Speaking—the "oral" approach—would require fitting Sophia with hearing aids and working with her to listen and speak. With the proper technology in place, Sophia would in theory *hear* all or at least most of the sounds I'd been grieving over. We would communicate with her in our native, spoken language. And she would learn to converse with the 99.98 percent of people who speak. The biggest risk with this approach was that she might not succeed in acquiring spoken language quickly or at all: we would not know for months whether the hearing aids and speech work provided her adequate access to spoken language. Without Sign to ensure the acquisition of *concepts* in this time period, she might be delayed, not just in language, but in *thought*.

For weeks on end, we mulled over our options, read articles, spoke to, and emailed as many people as we could. A decision didn't come to us all at once. But two separate conversations tipped us both toward the oral approach. Our friend Ian worked in a law firm with a deaf woman. Apparently, her hearing loss was the same severity as Sophia's. She grew up wearing hearing aids, and her parents worked with her concertedly on speech and spoken language. From Ian's account, the woman spoke very well and she was highly successful at work. From the woman's own account—we initiated contact with her over e-mail— she was living a very happy life, with a loving partner, a productive career, strong friendships, and an unhampered sense of opportunity.

Soon after our contact with her, we met an old friend of Bill's we hadn't seen in years. Over coffee, we described Sophia's situation and the decision we faced. The friend turned to Bill:

"Aren't you a lawyer now?"

Bill answered, "Yes."

"And you're a philosopher?" he asked me.

"Yes," I said.

"You two are TALKERS, aren't you?"

"And Jennifer's a singer, too," Bill added.

"Well, shouldn't you consider all that?"

From inside the "camps" of deafness—the "Signing" camp, the "Oral" camp—we often encountered a one-size-fits-all militancy. Now we considered the precise contours of Sophia's hearing loss, the particular features of our family. Bill and I were talkers. We were constantly debating, questioning, arguing, doubting, agreeing, wondering aloud. And we were hearers, in the hearing world. A soundless, wordless world was unimaginable to us. The audiologist had touted the latest digital hearing aids: they could be set to the exact dimensions of Sophia's hearing loss, programmed to amplify spoken language and to block out background noise. With this technology and speech work, there was a solid chance that Sophia could be trained to listen and speak. We could start right away.

Bill and I became convinced—or we convinced ourselves—to try the "oral approach" with Sophia. We could always re-evaluate, or switch to Sign, if we saw delays in Sophia's language capacities.

Was it self-centeredness? Could we not fathom our baby in a world other than our own? Or selfishness—was it our own need for intimacy that guided us? We didn't know. We were Sophia's parents and our world was hers. We told ourselves that we could afford a trial period.

◆ ◆ ◆

I draped Sophia over my still-slackened womb as the audiologist pumped bright blue stuff—gooey silicon that looked like saltwater taffy—into Sophia's ears to make earmold impressions for hearing aids. "Is it cold?" I pantomimed a shiver. Sophia's eyebrows splayed wide.

The hearing aids were huge, and they flopped off Sophia's tiny, three-month-old ears. The first day we put them in at home, tentatively wedging the earmolds into place and tucking the aids behind Sophia's ears, they whistled non-stop for an hour, until one of us finally pulled them out. The "feedback" came because Sophia was still too young to sit up, and whenever she leaned against anything—her crib mattress, her infant seat, the couch, the floor—the trapped sound traveled back into the microphone and was amplified again. After much experimentation, we found the baby carrier—with Sophia right up against one of our chests—to be our best solution: it held her head upright, so her hearing aids stopped whistling, and she was in close proximity to our speaking voices. Our first words, as soon as the aids were in: "We love you, Sophia."

I spoke into Sophia's ears—"miked" at top volume— and I wondered, did Pearl try stubbornly, ineffectually, to speak to her girls even after she knew of their deafness? Did she persist in speaking the words she deemed most crucial into their unfixable ears? And did her girls hear her, if not through the sound waves, then through the contours of her face, through her expressions? I kept my eyes fixed on Sophia so she might read my expressions. Just in case my sound wasn't getting through.

In time, our pockets would be filled with toupee tape, strings, clips, and rubber bands—anything that might keep the hearing aids in Sophia's ears long enough for her to hear a bit of spoken language each day. A read-through of *Good Night Moon*. A rendition of "When Cows Wake Up In The Morning, They Always Say 'Good Day.'" Each day, we worked with Sophia on listening with her hearing aids. We no longer ignored the hum of the refrigerator, or the sizzling of a frying egg; we pointed out the crinkling leaves, the approach of footsteps, every faucet run of water. "I hear it," I'd say and point to my ear, when the bed creaked, or a dog barked.

Did *she* hear it? I didn't know. I was half-reassured just by our having chosen a plan of action; half-terrified that it was a misguided one. I talked to Sophia constantly now. I narrated every activity and named every object in our path.

I interjected signs here and there. I admired, even craved, sign language the more I learned it. You couldn't turn away, stare off, do a thousand other things. It required presence and intimacy.

I took Sophia's hearing aids out for bath-time. In bathroom surround-sound, I alone heard the droplets of water drip from her short hair, the swishes and waves made by her kicks, the lap-lap of the water at the tub's edge. Did she wonder what the water sounded like? *Could* she wonder it? I toweled her off, and put the hearing aids back in her ears. Holding her suspended above the bathwater, I grabbed a handful and let it drip drip drip into the tub.

At night, Bill and I cradled Sophia in our arms and swayed to the rhythms of lullabies played far louder than lullabies ought to be. We had discs of lullabies from around the world: lilting voices from Tahiti; sharp operatic sopranos from Japan; gentle wooings from Israel.

When Sophia's eyes fluttered to close, we plied her with kisses and laid her down. Just before taking out her hearing aids, we'd whisper, "Bye, bye sound," and wave good night.

California, November 2000

EACH MORNING, I GENTLY WRIGGLED Sophia's hearing aids into her tiny ears. It stung me to see other mothers whispering softly in their babies' ears, their babies responding with gurgles and coos and pudgy fingers tapping at their mothers' lips. At the library, at the bookstore—mothers reading stories in airy, lilting voices; their children leaning in to listen, ready to catch magic. I couldn't afford whispers with Sophia. I spoke loudly, with the sharp enunciation of a strict grammar school teacher. The gentlest nursery rhyme, the sweetest lullaby, I now belted out at full volume—a bull in the china shop of motherese.

Only after Sophia's birth did I start to view my own childhood through the lens of my mother's hearing loss. I hadn't before traced my experience—the feeling that I wasn't being heard—to the dislocation in my mother's own upbringing, to the ways she grew up unhearing, and also, unheard. Nor had I traced it to the constant punking-out of my mother's hearing aid batteries. I began to wonder, in new motherhood, how it must have been for my mother with her hearing loss. I began to wonder how it was for Pearl—how she managed to moor her girls, so that they could in time tie a string from their wrists to their babies'. Awaken in the silence. How *I* might manage it.

◆ ◆ ◆

Bill and I started researching oral-deaf schools. Several schools had early infant programs to work with deaf babies and their parents on listening and vocalizing.

We went to a school in commuting distance one morning. We walked through the classrooms, then observed a preschool group through a one-way mirror inside a soundproof booth. Teachers drilled the students military-style. The children were just four or five years old, yet their foreheads tensed with effort. Their eyes pierced with concentration. They sputtered single-syllable sounds like "bah" and "pah"—sounds devoid of meaning. Not a single one of them was *speaking*. In the play area, they puttered about, lonely, each child in a bubble of isolation.

In the parking lot, I gasped for cool air and burst into tears.

"This is not the only school." Bill said. He must have felt as I did. "We can look around. We can look around the country."

"Really?"

We hadn't spoken about moving. People in the juvenile court had recently encouraged Bill to apply to be the new commissioner. It was a dream of Bill's to judge dependency cases. We both knew that if he were to get the job, he would be busy day and night. Now, my head swirled with the prospect of relocating.

On the computer the next morning, I found sites for every oral school in the country. I followed up with calls. I had an instant rapport with the director of the parent-infant program at the oldest school, the Clarke School for the Deaf in Northampton, Massachusetts. Her name was Jan, and her perspective on deaf education was rooted in a rich study of child development. She asked about our bonding with Sophia, about our style of play. I phoned Bill at work, my voice full of excitement. He suggested we arrange a visit.

I jumped in the shower, thinking about all the conversations I'd had that morning. My hands and hair were lathered thick with apricot shampoo when I panicked. Before my shower, I had placed Sophia, asleep, in the middle of the bed—she was safe there—but I hadn't closed the door.

What if Lucca jumped up onto the bed and squashed her? I rushed out of the shower, blotting foam from my forehead, and sprinted down the hallway.

I heard Lucca's tail thumping the bedcovers before I saw her. Up on the bed, Lucca's body curled like a horseshoe around Sophia, who was still sound asleep. Dripping wet, I kissed Lucca's snout, praised her, and ran back into the shower to rinse.

◆ ◆ ◆

Days before our flight east to visit the Clarke School, I located a US Census Report from 1930 listing Nellie Wertheim living with her daughter Bertha on Union Street in Brooklyn. I also located army registration forms for Nellie's sons, Manny and Leo, and I found a phone number for my cousin, Valerie. Valerie was interested in our family tree, too. She'd been working on a different branch of it—the Meyer line—over the course of several years, since her mother died. She'd met with relatives this past summer to learn what she could. I told her of my efforts to learn about Pearl and Moshe Wertheim, and their daughters, Nellie and Bayla.

Valerie told me of ways to search through birth and marriage certificates, immigration documents, holocaust records, and synagogue membership lists. I mentioned the asterisks near some of the names on the family chart, and my interest in our family's deafness. I described how I'd located Nellie in US Census Reports, but not Bayla, and how I hoped to find the whereabouts of Judith Fleischer, perhaps our one living deaf relative.

Valerie must have heard the weariness in my voice, because she offered to help. She started to write out a list.

As Valerie ticked off concrete search strategies—we could search student rosters at schools for the deaf and TTY directories; we could look at boat schedules and Ellis Island records—I despaired of ever learning how Nellie and Bayla really lived, how they *fared*. Their names scrawled on school attendance sheets—what would those tell me of the rhythm of their days, their nights? Fragmented images swirled in my head. Half-hidden faces, one cheek cold against the white plaster wall. Two eyes flickering in a candle-flame's shadow, yellow against the dark brocaded drapery. Were our deaf ancestors shunned, kept out of view? Did they sneak sunshine upon their pale faces only when no one was looking?

All afternoon, I wanted to phone Valerie back. To explain how I perched precariously in new motherhood, in search of models, in search of ties. How I grew up groundless amidst the static of interrupted connections, how I nursed only fractured childhood memories. Fish flopping on the lawn after a rainstorm flooded the pond. The smell of clover by the old railroad ties. Violin music. The tiny vials of oil from a perfume-making kit. My father's mittenless hands shaking with chill as he buckled up my ski boots. My mother's expression, laid bare like wet seaglass, as I sang to her. That laid-bare expression, recollecting itself, as if for departure. The heat of the kitchen. The din of family voices. The force of loneliness that could have replaced gravity itself.

I knew that my questions—*Were Nellie and Bayla known? Did anyone push through the barrier of their deafness to know them?*—were unanswerable. I sat down on the quilted glider in the nursery and held Sophia snug to my chest. I thought about my mother, how she retreated daily to her mirror, hid behind the closed bathroom door. She had been bereft in childhood. I didn't know the particular circumstances of her father's leaving. Yet now I pictured her as a girl, scuttling down four flights of fire stairs, watching his car pull away, a smudge of black on grey. I pictured her tottering back up the stairs, then coming to stand at the bathroom mirror, shaky, with eyeliner and mascara in hand. Trying to conceal her tears, to makeup her eyes. Makeup: *make believe, invent.* Or: *cover over, camouflage.*

Throughout my own childhood, my mother's eyes—alternately cast on me, then turned away—always held her father's leaving. She identified with her father, he who had also been left, he who left her behind. I sought to retrieve her, yet my eyes, too, filled up with the look of departure. And now I clutched, unmoored, to my Sophia.

◆ ◆ ◆

In Massachusetts, Bill maneuvered our bright red rental car up a steep, narrow Northampton street, marked with an engraved metal placard for Clarke School for the Deaf. Signposts in the shape of yellow diamonds marked each crosswalk with the word "DEAF"—a descriptor I still couldn't weave into my thoughts about Sophia without an internal revolt.

Just a week before, back in California, we had brought Sophia to the audiologist for another hearing test and a review of her hearing aid settings. Her diagnosis was "severe" on a scale of mild, moderate, severe, and profound. I had stepped into the thick sound booth full of groundless hope: my girl would hear today, and her diagnosis, like a judge's sentence, would be lessened or even reversed. With Sophia, three and a half months old, cradled on my lap, I had sat completely still as my own ears filled with the sounds piped in, and I had waited for Sophia's ears to register the pure tones, for her eyes to widen with each beep. It was not the last time I would teeter out of a sound booth, crestfallen.

We parked on the street, the fresh air a relief after the artificial cherry scent of the rental car. Bill looked at maps of Northampton and Amherst while I nursed Sophia. An extra feeding, because she wasn't gaining weight fast enough.

Toting Sophia in her infant seat, we toured the Clarke preschool. The classroom was cheery and bright, and the children were playing—really playing. They had a make-believe lemon tree and a lemonade stand. They were squeezing, tasting, puckering, sugaring, stirring, pouring. They were buying and selling. They were talking!

"You want lemonade?"

"Yes. Ooh. That sour."

"Want sugar?"

"Yes! I pour it myself. Here my money."

We observed the preschool for over an hour. From within the observation booth, we listened in with headphones to the wondrous sound of deaf children talking! Some more advanced than others; some in need of intense prompting. But all of them talking, and all of them *playing*. Afterward, we drove around Northampton's neighborhoods with a real estate booklet. We gawked at turn-of-the-century houses that we could actually afford, then ate decent

Tandoori at an Indian restaurant while Sophia slept in her infant seat under our table.

We returned to the Clarke School to meet with Jan, the director of the parent-infant program I had spoken to by phone. Jan had a light in her eyes even brighter than the fuschia hair ribbon she wore to dazzle her young charges. She greeted us warmly and spoke with enthusiasm about child development, parental bonding, and play. She led us through the school, founded in the 1860s, before even Nellie was born. Jan, herself, had worked at Clarke for almost thirty years.

By now Sophia was wide awake. We settled ourselves on the floor in Jan's office and played with Sophia as we had grown accustomed. We sounded off toys by rattling maracas, squeaking a rubber cat, or pressing a fuzzy duck for its quack, then made a big show by widening our eyes, pointing to our ears, and proclaiming "I hear it" in response to each sound. Jan watched us for a long while. Eventually, she spoke up:

"Sophia is going to be fine, no matter what school or what communication method you choose. You may decide to come here. But you needn't move all the way from California. Sophia is alert and engaged. Above all, you are connected—you are an intact family."

I felt my body relax into the floor as Jan spoke. Her

words loosened the muscles that had knotted in my guts, and I breathed deeply for the first time in three months. Jan had worked with deaf children and their families her entire professional life. Child development was her life's passion. She said Sophia was going to be fine.

◆ ◆ ◆

On the plane ride back to California, Bill told me he had decided not to apply for the commissioner position. Sophia was the priority now. We talked about moving to Northampton. We agreed that if we were in the right place to raise Sophia, the other facets of our lives would work out. The Clarke School, and Northampton, felt promising to both of us. We decided to launch job searches in western Massachusetts, and when at least one of us found sustainable employment, we'd move.

When we arrived home from the Northampton trip, one of the messages waiting on our voicemail system was from my cousin Valerie. I dialed her back before we had lugged the last of our bags into the entryway. Bill shot me an annoyed look. I motioned to Sophia, fast asleep in her infant car seat, a justification for returning the phone call now rather than later.

"Jennifer, I think I found a death record for Judith Fleischer."

I was struck, silent.

"Jennifer, are you there?" Valerie asked.

"Are you sure it's *our* Judith Fleischer?" I sputtered.

I hadn't known until that moment how desperately I had hoped to meet her, possibly my one remaining deaf ascendant. How I had placed my hopes for understanding my family's deaf past—and for navigating my family's future—on the stories I believed she alone could tell me.

◆ ◆ ◆

That night, I sat at my desk and tried to finish writing a philosophy paper that I had started before Sophia was born. For over an hour, while Bill and Sophia slept, I stared at my computer screen and tried to make sense of my now incomprehensible academic writing. I rifled through reference books and related philosophy articles. I turned arguments over and over in my head. It was no use.

I reached for a new novel, one I had bought the same day as I'd bought the blank journal. *The River Midnight*, by Lilian Nattel, about life in an imaginary shtetl called Blaszka. Part of my new research program.

"Time grows short at the end of a century, like winter days when night falls too soon. In the dusk, angels and demons

— 77 —

walk. Who knows who they are? Or which is which. But there they are, sneaking their gifts into the crevices of change . . ."

I moved myself to the living room couch and spread a fleecy blanket on top of me. In no time, I was lost in the jabber of the market square, the heat of the tavern, the swallows of mushroom soup that kept December's early chill at bay.

◆ ◆ ◆

Bill and I started our job searches. I bypassed the official, academic job market and instead had my dossier sent to the five colleges in the vicinity of Northampton—Smith, Mount Holyoke, Hampshire, Amherst, and UMass Amherst. During Sophia's nap time, I typed up cover letters, trying to sound engaged and committed to my scholarly work.

Surrounding me on all sides, our floor-to-ceiling bookshelves held tome after mighty tome of the great Western philosophers. In graduate school, I revered these books. I believed that they spoke to me. But now, they were silent. Just theoretical musings for minds detached from the reality of new babies, of my baby. Some were worse than silent:

disparaging of the languageless deaf, deemed incapable of thought.

When I had started graduate work, I had fixed on the riddles that went to my core: the metaphysics of nothing, the empty set—did it not swell, like a wet cardboard box, full with its emptiness? And skepticism, the question of whether you can ever know another mind, or be known by another? If the holes, generations-deep, wouldn't fill, I could at least stare them down into abstractions.

Bishop Berkeley's phrase: *esse est percipi* (to be is to be perceived) had brought me to my knees. Not because of an enchantment with idealism. It stirred me like poetry, ratifying my sense of a tenuous existence, of having grown up largely unperceived. *Esse est percipi*. It transported me back to my mother's bathroom countertop, my little-girl thighs sticking to the cold yellow tile. Rows of wicker baskets brimming with compacts, lipsticks, curling pins. The smell of hairspray. I watched my mother lean into the mirror, rail thin and powdery, her frantic eyes chasing after a vanishing girl. Looking too long. Longing.

"Mom?"

Her mascara-coated eyelashes made short black streaks on the glass.

If my mother saw me, it was through her reflection, her

projection. I was fractured, as if by a prism, or a multi-fold mirror, and the parts of me that failed to match her self-image were cut away from view, unseen. I tried my best to become like her, to garner the light of her gaze, with dress, with song.

When I first started taking voice lessons in New York City, my mother sometimes accompanied me. We'd order the French onion soup at O'Neals' Balloon. Then we'd stroll along the Lincoln Center streets, and I'd sing to her.

"*Ah fors'e lui che l'anima*"—my favorite aria from *La Traviata*, it often felt like my best chance for connection with my mother. From the time I was fifteen until the time I left for college, my singing of its lines—"*A quell l'a mor, quell l'a mor ch'e palpito, del l'universo, del l'universo intero*"— could render my mother focused and attentive, her eyes huge, her lips quivering. Her heart unburied.

The last lines, the song's climax, became my deepest regret. My mother's attentions would flicker, and I would again be prone to the intermittencies, the inconsistencies, that marked my childhood and destabilized me. My prized creations—a lopsided pot of colored clay, a woven lanyard bracelet, pages of schoolwork marked "excellent"— celebrated, then discarded in the trash. A birthday one year filled with fanfare, the next, nearly forgotten. A question, unanswered. Unheard.

As I left home for college—I went to Columbia, planning to continue with my voice lessons on Sixty-sixth Street—I wavered uncertainly, a chalk mark on the verge of being erased. Along with singing, philosophy became my way to cast myself, to hurtle myself into the world. What are the elements essential for identity, for personhood, for perception and existence? If a tree falls in the forest and no one is there to hear it, does it make a sound?

I met Bill in the law library on a damp April evening during my junior year. He was a first year law student. We talked and talked—first in the library, then at a pub, then on Columbia's main steps—Bill's eyes holding me securely in his gaze all the while. When we parted that night at the huge iron doorway to my building, I loved him already. His eyelids crinkled around his soft blue eyes and his cheeks dimpled when he smiled at me through the grated window. My belly fluttered as I weaved up the six flights of stairs to my dorm room, and fell, joyously, into sleep.

That summer, swimming together in a lake, Bill lifted me up with his strong forearms and swished me around, weightless. We made up silly rhymes about New York Mets baseball players—Jesse Orosco, Dwight Goodin, Gary Carter—and I sang him snippets of songs from *The Fantasticks* in between dives that I took from off his broad shoulders. Toweled and warmed by the sun, we sat with our legs still dangling in the water and passed a container of coffee ice cream back and forth. Bill's tee shirt smelled like the corn plant that flowered in his apartment, and I nestled my face into his shoulder. When he swept me up in a hug, I could hardly breathe for the strength he brought, his arms braced tight around me.

Over the next twelve years, we'd move to northern California, I'd pursue my PhD, we'd marry, have a baby. Bill's steady eyes held me, even now. But I quivered still. To be is to be perceived. I questioned whether I had presence enough for him, for Sophia.

◆ ◆ ◆

We landed east coast jobs. Bill was hired to work in a children's law clinic in Hartford, Connecticut, a forty-five minute drive from Northampton. His position had teaching and supervision components at an affiliated law school. I was hired to teach half-time in Mount Holyoke's philosophy department: Introduction to Philosophy and whatever I wanted for an upper level seminar. I began devising a seminar called Complexities of the Self about how we can be divided, deceived, and opaque even to ourselves. I'd been interested, since my dissertation days, in the relevant philosophical topics—weakness of will, wishful thinking, self-deception. And now there was my own burgeoning obsession dividing me between the present and the past, between memory and invention.

I was consumed with my deaf ancestry. With little hope of uncovering detailed information through family stories or genealogical research, I now found myself *inventing* scenarios, conjuring imaginary tales about my great-great aunts. Thinking of Nellie and Bayla, I wondered: was I somehow inoculating myself to my worst fears for Sophia? Was I vying for control over *others'* fates, even if not our own? Was I simply diverting my attention, a break from the stressors of life? Whatever the reason, thinking of them comforted me somehow. Quieted me.

◆ ◆ ◆

Bill and I searched the Northampton housing market via the web. We found a one hundred-year-old house just a few blocks away from the Clarke School. I pictured us in that neighborhood, pushing Sophia in her stroller beneath a canopy of huge maple trees, Lucca bounding by our sides.

I flew out to see the house. It had wavy glass windows and thick detailed moldings, a fireplace and beautiful wood floors. In winter, we could snuggle with Sophia in front of the fire, reading board books and playing games. We could introduce her to snow—we didn't get any in the Bay area. We could teach her to sled and skate, to ski and build snow-men. In fall, we could gather red, orange, and yellow leaves, and iron them between sheets of wax paper. And we could stroll through the Smith College gardens in spring and summer, set out picnics at Paradise Pond. Except for the busy wallpaper and wall-to-wall carpet in every bedroom, it was perfect. Bill said he trusted my judgment, so we bid on the house and bought it, for him sight-unseen.

I had packed my journal for the trip. I'd been writing in it most nights. Whole story lines about Pearl and her daughters—story lines that always ended with strings, wrist to wrist. Then a baby's cry, a soft tug-tug on the line, and a mother awakening to her child.

On the flight back to California, I pulled the journal from my handbag, slowly unwinding the string that held its pages closed tight. Despite all my search efforts, I had just the two Census Reports of 1910 and 1930 showing Nellie in Brooklyn, first on State Street, and later on Union Street with her daughter, Bertha. And I had the army registration forms for her sons, Manny and Leo. I still had nothing on Bayla, nothing on Pearl or Moshe. I had no sense of how my ancestors really fared day to day, how they lived in deaf-ness amidst the other challenges of the times.

I *needed* these ancestors. I needed them for guidance. I needed them for company. I needed them for escape.

In my writing, my own anxieties and hopes entwined with those whose existences I couldn't flesh out in the light of day. My ancestors were becoming real to me, if only in my mind, and I latched onto them.

Galicia, 1871

CAUTIOUSLY AT FIRST, *joy sneaks its way past the evil eye, into the house. Nellie's baby-charms—her curled pink toes, her shock of black hair—soften even the deep furrows in Moshe's brow. And such eyes! Dark and penetrating.*

In time, Pearl will brag that Nellie sees like an eagle. Nearly two, she can find every last button Pearl hides in a hide and seek game. But so stubborn, and she refuses to obey! "Look at her," Pearl scoffs, as Nellie scooches her way across the threshold and out toward the chicken coop, even as Pearl and now Moshe call to her to stop.

Pearl can feel Nellie's eyes searching her face when she picks her up roughly from among the chickens and pulls bits of straw from her hair. "You must come when we call out to you. Who can run a house this way?" Pearl plops Nellie down on her bed, the room dim and shadowy grey, then walks out.

A minute later, she comes back. Nellie is fingering the damask bedspread and she startles at Pearl's appearance, every muscle tensed like a spooked animal. Pearl turns to look over her shoulder. What on earth is the matter? She grabs up Nellie and holds her to her cheek.

◆ ◆ ◆

At night beneath that same damask spread, Pearl lies awake, staring at the ceiling. She knows—has known for months— that something is wrong with her child. Nearly two years old, and Nellie doesn't speak yet. Well, she might be a late bloomer with that. But the expression on Nellie's face earlier today, so surprised and confused when Pearl reappeared in the bedroom . . . as if she hadn't heard Pearl coming, hadn't heard her calls, hadn't heard her chidings, or later, her consoling words.

All the next day Pearl wanders about in a fog, consumed with her worries about Nellie. How could she have failed to notice? Nellie spends her days scanning the house for clues of activity, laying her palms and occasionally even her broad cheek flat on the floor with the approach of footsteps. Now Pearl calls out for Nellie from behind. No head turn. Now she clangs two pans together. Nothing. No.

When Moshe walks in at sundown with four unexpected guests for Shabbat dinner, Pearl is beside herself. Must the mitzvah of hospitality be theirs to make, tonight of all nights? Pearl wants to excuse herself from the packed living room and somehow prepare Nellie for the crowd. But Moshe is already calling for Nellie in a voice louder than usual. He is walking room to room, pounding on the walls as he walks. Pearl wonders who these guests are, why Moshe is making such a show. He smells of the rabbi's chamber.

Pearl backs out of the room and rushes down the hall past Moshe. She finds Nellie at her bedroom window, a dollop of lantern light shining on the rag doll in her hand. Pearl hoists Nellie up and gestures that it is time to eat. Moshe stands in her path, as she scurries toward the kitchen.

"What is the matter with that child?"

"We'll talk later, after dinner."

"No. I want to talk now."

"Moshe, we have guests standing around the table."

Later, when Moshe runs his finger along the base of Pearl's neck as she tidies up after dinner, she jerks away. She turns to look into his face, and for a moment she flashes with what power she has, to withhold herself, to withhold her news. Moshe pales, suddenly. "What is it, Pearl? You glow and you glower at the same time."

"Nellie is a good girl. She is not disobedient. Not on purpose."

"She is disobedient. She doesn't listen."

"She doesn't hear, Moshe. She can't hear."

"What are you talking about? Of course she hears."

"No, Moshe."

"She meets me at the door almost every afternoon when I come home. How does she know I am coming if she can't hear?"

"She feels it in the ground. I'm telling you, she doesn't hear."

◆ ◆ ◆

In the rabbi's study, lines of thought are pushed and pulled, twisted and turned. Voices rise and fall. Eyes are rubbed; beards are tugged. Questions are always answered with other questions.

If it can be said that any of the men in the rabbi's study are practical, the practical one among them—Chaim—stands up and looks at the others.

"Can she be married?" he asks, his eyebrows arched high.

"She's two years old," says Yaacov the candlemaker, with a dismissive wave of his blistered hands. "You're asking, can she be married?"

"I'm asking, yes, because Pearl and Moshe are worried. They want to know: what kind of life can she expect to live? Can she be married, have a family?"

"Why not, if a match was to be accepted?" Yitzchak the trader offers.

"Well," inserts Shmuele, the scholar, "the Mishnah makes distinctions: there are the deaf who cannot speak, cannot reason intellectually or morally; and the deaf who can. If she is the former, she will be forever like a child."

"Moshe says she hasn't spoken a word yet," Chaim mutters, as if only to himself.

"But there is a chance, no? that she will recover," Yitzchak puts in. "She is only two years old, and for her age, she watches intently. Besides, she needn't become an orator, just to become a bride."

A deaf baby girl in their midst. The scholars and sages of Tasse are unsure of what to think. To abide by the ancient texts, Pearl and Moshe's baby might as well be a corpse. A cheresh, deaf and mute, lacks cognition, the basis of a person's status. Luckily, some in the room, including the rabbi himself, have traveled to Budapest and witnessed deaf people conversing with their hands. If the deaf can talk with their hands, maybe they have some thoughts in their heads.

An argument can be built, no? In any case, it needn't be so strong. Nellie is a girl, sweet and pretty. How many thoughts does she need? And if she doesn't talk so much, well, when it comes to marrying, a man might consider himself lucky.

Pearl sits on the bench outside, shifting, then re-shifting her weight, shaking out her legs. Her belly is enormous already, and the mole on her neck is bigger, darker. Moshe paces back and forth, back and forth, brushing away a low tree branch that tangles his hair with each pass.

When the door of the rabbi's house opens, it is declared that Nellie can honor her community with mitzvoth the same as any other girl. Pearl heaves a sigh of relief, and stands to take Moshe's hand. But Moshe's hand is limp; his eyes don't meet hers. Moshe can sense the retreat of the men. As they file out of the rabbi's front door, their downcast eyes ooze the permanent liquid of pity.

It is different with the women. In time, the women open up to Pearl with stories—a deaf cousin in London, a deaf niece in Vienna. They bring news of schools in London, Berlin, and Budapest run exclusively for the deaf. They bounce Nellie on their knees, exaggerated expressions on their faces. And the women come to crowd around Pearl in her newest labor, to stand strong as she leans and groans and squats, to wring out towels with clean water.

But when Pearl holds her second daughter in her arms, and recognizes in her new baby's eyes the already-focused stare of eagles, she asks the women to please leave her, to go, to go.

Pearl looks into the living room. Moshe is sitting with a book. His face is disgruntled and his fingers are wound tight with the white fringes that stick out beneath his shirt. Nellie is standing at the crib, peering through the slatted rails. She is studying her baby sister, asleep with her legs bent like a frog's, her arms stretched straight above her head. Pearl goes to Nellie. She points to the baby, and struggles to explain that she cannot hear. Moshe grouses loudly from his reading chair—"you don't know that"—but Pearl is certain. She knows the scanning eyes, the searching fingertips, the flattening palms against the floor. She points to Nellie's ears, then to Bayla's, and shakes her head "no."

Moshe rustles himself out of the living room chair and shuts himself off in his study. Pearl counts to herself. Five months since Bayla's birth, and Moshe still hasn't come to her in the night. Not that she's so eager. These nights, she does the extra baking once Nellie and Bayla finally sleep. Her hair, damp from the mikva, she wraps up into a tight knot under her marriage wig. Why should she advertise her monthly cycles, marked out by her trips to the bath house? God knows she is trying to be a good wife, a good mother. So, why? She begs God to tell her, why this curse of daughters who cannot hear?

At the market, in the upstairs galley of the shul, at the river to collect water, Pearl watches other mothers with their children, and she knows it is different for them. They sing to their young ones in breathy whispers, in octave-leaping coos. They invent stories, and the children's eyes grow wide. A calf in an imaginary flower-drenched meadow takes its first wobbly steps. A silvery fish breaks through a lake's shimmering surface to speak in magical tongues. A ball of yarn mysteriously appears in an old peddler's basket. Stories Nellie and Bayla will never hear.

Pearl falters in fits and starts, in a confused pantomime, trying to understand and meet her little girls' most immediate needs and desires. Bayla cries and Pearl offers her more to eat, hands her a doll to play with, and then sees—oh!—her little finger is red and swollen, it must have gotten pinched in the slats of the crib.

Nellie's hungry eyes devour everything in their sight. Yet, Pearl can see that the patterns of days and weeks do not compose a familiar rhythm for Nellie. Routine events—the frenzied buying on market day, the lighting of the braided Havdalah candle—come as a surprise, a new enchantment to Nellie week after week after week. Pearl's fears mingle, then, with the thrill of her girl's endless, childlike wonder. At least with Bayla's arrival, Nellie no longer sits alone, hours on end, in the nook beneath her bedroom windowsill. She rushes about the house and cares for Bayla. She helps Pearl bathe her. She strokes her fuzzy scalp. She fusses over her clothes. Pearl watches from the kitchen as Nellie gently rocks Bayla in her crib, its wooden rails suspended from strong ropes that run from the ceiling. Nellie gestures and points, makes faces and whole body movements. Her face is alight, like a well-lit house on a dark night.

Massachusetts, May 2001

SOPHIA WAS TEN MONTHS OLD when we arrived in Northampton. Light flooded into our house through the huge, wavy glass windowpanes. Bill and I arranged for modest home renovations: we had the busy wallpaper removed and each room painted in a deep, historic color.

In the spirit of my superstitious forebears, I hung a *chamsa*, a "protecting hand," from the iron doorknob in our front entryway. Sophia ran her little fingers over the glistening hand, molded in shiny copper and bejeweled in brilliant turquoise, the "eye" in the center meant to ward off evil. Despite our modernity, the strategy of averting trouble through an ancient stare down still held its appeal.

Jan came to our house from the Clarke School the first week, and every week from then on. She brought huge tote bags filled with toys and visual props to accompany songs to sing and books to read: itsy bitsy spiders and waterspouts, five little monkeys and doctors and beds, a plastic

Humpty Dumpty egg, a stuffed toy rat and a sack of malt, and the house that Jack built.

Together with Jan, we sat on the floor of our living room and engaged in "auditory-play therapy" with Sophia. We set up a toy car on a track, and as it ran we said "go!" We tucked a doll into a miniature bed, then nudged it and called out, "Wake up, baby!"

Jan taught us to narrate everything we were doing, and to take extra care to prepare Sophia for what was happening with both visual and auditory cues. Before a car ride we were to bring our keys to Sophia, show them to her, and jangle them near her ear. Before a bath, we were to carry Sophia to the tub, show her the running water, and let her hear it. It might be typical for all babies, especially those who nap often, to expect the unexpected, or else to be beset by confusion: they fall asleep, they wake up in the supermarket; they fall back asleep, they wake up in Florida in Grandma's living room. But deaf children are at risk for confusion even when they are awake because they miss the auditory cues that tell hearing children what will happen next. A dog's bark + heavy footsteps down the hall + a deep voice trailing in = Daddy's home. Without the anticipatory sounds, Daddy appears as if from thin air.

Multiple times each day, Sophia pulled out her hearing aids. She'd reach behind her ears, yank the aids off, and throw them across the room or drop them into her bowl of oatmeal or plunge them into her mouth. Jan was insistent that the aids be returned to Sophia's ears immediately after the necessary clean up.

We had other concerns by now, too, one that even overshadowed the hearing loss. Sophia's weight was low—so low that doctors labeled her with the term "failure to thrive." She had never eaten a lot, and even the move to solid foods hadn't boosted her weight. At birth she had been in the fiftieth percentile, and now she was below the first. Specialists urged us to consider feeding Sophia with tubes—a nasalgastric tube run down her nose, or a G-tube surgically inserted into her stomach. We resisted such invasive measures, and tried fattening her up the old fashioned way. We put cream into everything we served her, trying to make each bite as calorie-rich as possible. We ate at busy restaurants to keep her distracted as we nudged morsels of muffin, bites of ziti, or spoonfuls of vanilla ice cream into her mouth. We bought every high-calorie food we could think of to entice her to eat. Maple butter, tapioca pudding, strawberry cheesecake. Once I prevailed upon a baker to sell me a container full of cannoli filling. Most of our "hearing lessons" had baking and eating components. All of us *but* Sophia grew fatter—Bill and I ate cheesecake in middle-of-the-night fits of stress, and Lucca gobbled up every last bit that fell uneaten from Sophia's high chair.

Early on, Jan recommended that we create picture books for Sophia: "where" books and "who" books to provide Sophia with visual narratives of our days. For a week, I kept a camera in the car and snapped pictures to document our routines. The following Saturday, I sat at our kitchen table, spooning strained peaches (and cream) into Sophia's mouth and squash soup into mine. An orange meal for both of us. Then I set out the developed pictures, back from the camera shop, and began to organize them before placing them in transparent pouches. *Sophia at the pediatrician's office; Sophia in the audiology booth; Sophia in a lesson with Jan.* As I considered what order to put them in, I was overcome by a sudden revulsion, a desire to throw them all out. Where was *Sophia at the playground, Sophia at the children's library, Sophia at a friend's house?* The only pictures unrelated to Sophia's therapies were pictures of the restaurants and supermarkets we frequented. I flashed with anger, first at our circumstances, then at myself. Why had I let Sophia's young life become narrowed in this way? Why hadn't I rounded out her therapy schedule and medical appointments with diversions, playdates, fun outings?

The next morning I took pictures of the public library, a nearby park, and a playground. Over the next few days, we photographed children Sophia was becoming friendly with. Ben, with a big smile on his face and a flower-puppet in his hand. Katie, with a colorful dress-up scarf billowing like a wizard's cape around her shoulders. Julia, gnawing on a gigantic ear of corn. Bill took a picture of Sophia and me whooshing down a slide. We dug out photographs of our extended family and family friends. I put them all in Sophia's albums, vowing to plan (and to narrate) richer, fuller days with Sophia.

◆ ◆ ◆

From Northampton, we were two hours away from my parents in Connecticut. Every three or four weeks, we would drive down to see them or they would come up to spend the afternoon with us. My mother devised fattening recipes for me to try on Sophia, using ricotta cheese and mascarpone. My father collected newspaper clippings, sometimes about deafness or low weight, sometimes about a philosopher or a psychologist whose work I might find interesting. I was glad to be nearer to my parents—I wanted a steady connection with them as much as ever.

When Bill traveled for work, I would stay over at my parents' with Sophia. Early on, I would watch apprehensively as my parents interacted with Sophia, fearful that

Sophia's wide open gaze would go unmet as my parents' attentions turned to other things—dressing, reading a day's newspaper, preparing a too-extravagant meal. I would stand by, ready to catch Sophia's felled gaze in mine. To my relief, my parents played with Sophia attentively. Both my father and my mother doted on her, but my mother communed with Sophia. Calm and focused, she gave Sophia her full attention—attention I had experienced, *cherished*, only in fleeting, intermittent intervals as a child.

With Sophia in her lap, my mother compared their hearing aids. She favored Sophia's soft, rubbery, colorful earmolds to her own hard, plastic, white ones. Once she noticed a red patch where Sophia's hearing aid had rubbed a raw spot behind her ear. Hurriedly, my mother brought out the baby oil and gently soothed Sophia's skin there. I watched them bond, eyes locked. Deafness shared. My mother combed Sophia's hair, tickled her cheeks. She made a high-calorie rice pudding, and Sophia ate it all up.

◆ ◆ ◆

As we went about our daily lives in Northampton, we didn't meet many deaf people. Our hearing lessons with Jan took place in our house, to support our listening practices at home. Bill and I made contact with some Clarke School parents, but there were no other deaf babies at Clarke then with whom to form a playgroup for Sophia. Most often, the hearing-impaired people we met were octogenarians rattling shopping carts slowly down the aisles of the supermarket. Sophia always noticed and pointed to their hearing aids, even the small beige ones that fit snugly inside their ears.

On occasion, I would see people Signing. And though we had opted for hearing aids and an oral approach for Sophia, I would find myself crossing streets, nearly jumping buses, in order to get a chance to introduce Sophia and to explain, in my halting sign language, that Sophia was hearing impaired, too. They would fawn over her, signing out her sweetness and beauty. Then they would face her directly and sign to her and she would stare back at them, absorbing their open expressions.

One day I saw two women, deaf and blind, signing into each other's hands. My thoughts ran me, then, to the setting sun on the Sabbath, no lanterns lit along the shtetl streets. The dusky shadows would have ended the possibility of further conversation for Nellie and Bayla—unless they took up each other's hands, as the deaf-blind do, and signed into each other's palms. I longed, then, to share in the hand language of the Deaf—Nellie and Bayla's home Sign, their only buffer from utter isolation. And I vowed to arm Sophia with everything the modern world would allow to make *her* less isolated, less vulnerable. A TTY system, if she couldn't talk on the phone. A vibrating alarm clock. A light-up smoke detector.

Surprisingly, the Deaf people we met didn't often challenge our decision to try hearing aids. It was the hearing people who subjected me to their questions, opinions, exclamations, and doubts. They stopped me on the street, in the pharmacy, at the coffee shop. "Why does your baby have hearing aids?" "Will she get better?" "Are you sure she needs those?" "What's wrong with her?"

There were days that I returned home exhausted from fielding questions, angry, and filled with self-doubt. What if Sophia wasn't really hearing spoken language with her hearing aids? Hearing aids amplified sound, but they did so *indiscriminately*—they amplified the hum of the fan or the rumble of a passing truck just as much they amplified speaking voices. And they did so *crudely*, making sounds louder, but not clearer, thus adding further distortion to Sophia's auditory process. The range of sound Sophia produced was narrow—high squeals and oohs— nothing like the rich babbling of babies, the sputterings of every possible language packed within. At ten months old, Sophia barely vocalized at all. And there was plenty of time each day when her hearing aids weren't even in her ears:

at bath-time, at nap-time, and at all the other times in the day when she pulled them out, poised to stuff them into her mouth.

I acquired an almost mystic ability to sense when Sophia was about to put an earmold in her mouth. Even in the car, when she sat behind me in her backward facing car seat, I knew. The drive to eat hearing technology—it deserves its own mention as a stage in oral development! I told myself it could be worse. At the Boston Children's Hospital, there was a large shadow box in the Otolaryngology waiting room that displayed all of the things surgeons had taken out of the ears, noses, and throats of children since the 1950s: fish hooks, nails, coins, open safety pins, and unidentifiable metal objects, some as big as nail clippers, each pinned into its allotted square with a typed description of the object, where in the body it was lodged, and when (and by whom) it was removed.

My fear that Sophia might choke on or swallow her hearing aids was matched only by my panic that we'd permanently lose them. They were expensive—over four thousand dollars—and she'd have to go weeks without hearing before they could be replaced. Sophia's newest favorite game, while we walked along forest paths with Lucca, was to throw her hearing aids into the woods from high up on her perch in my backpack. Their beige color made a perfect camouflage, and it sometimes took me hours, searching through leaves, retracing my steps, to find them.

Late at night, Bill and I would each take a toothpick and delicately pick out the mashed bananas, the dirt, and the carpet fuzz from her hearing aid microphones. The "silver lining" of Sophia's hearing loss was that when she slept unaided, we could be as loud as we wished: we could talk, we could shout, we could have friends over late into the night, we could have sex—so long as we didn't change the light. Sophia would wake to changes of light.

During Sophia's waking hours, I spent time focusing with her on single words, "power words" that could help her get things she wanted. *STOP* and *GO* and *MORE* and *ALL DONE*. I did the (incessant) talking: "*Do you want to OPEN the bag?; let's OPEN it; I'm OPENING the bag; see, I OPENED it.*" Every utterance I made felt loud, over-articulated, contrived, and repetitive.

Then one sunny summer morning, I sat Sophia in her blue and white striped high chair. Heavy cream filled her bottle and elbow noodles saturated with butter and cheese covered her tray. As usual, she was not much interested in eating. Instead she was all about testing me: looking right at me as I said "no," and hurling bits of pasta onto the floor.

And then I heard it:

"UP!"

"*What?* What did you say?"

"UP!"

I snatched her UP—her words *would* have power! I spun her around the kitchen, and called everyone I knew. Sophia's first word: "UP!" She was an optimist!

Then, just two days later: "OUT!"

A mover, a shaker! Sophia wanted UP and OUT!

And soon after, a long list of words: sock, cup, light, keys. And foods—so many foods—apple, pasta, banana, cheese, corn, soup—a happy byproduct of our obsessing over what (and how little) she ate. I wrote down every word she spoke on a bright pink page and placed it on our white refrigerator door.

◆ ◆ ◆

Sophia sported a curious Kentucky accent. And she spoke as if she frequented roadside fast food stands, asking for "hot doggies" and the like.

By the time Sophia was a year and a half old, she no longer pulled her hearing aids out; they were part of her. When she woke up, she pointed to her ears and then to the Dri Aid container where her hearing aids were stored over night. She *wanted* to hear, to be plugged into the sounds of the day. She knew nothing of our anxieties over whether her hearing loss was *progressive*—always a looming possibility that the audiologists monitored in the testing booth. We fretted, too, over Sophia's hearing aid settings. Three separate brainstem tests yielded three different audiograms, and we engaged in endless debates with the audiologists over how Sophia's hearing aids should be digitally programmed, given the discrepancies.

Despite our worries, Sophia's language capacities exploded. Our joy over her strides, her first words and expanded babbles, hit a high when Sophia muttered the word "shit" under her breath. With hearing aids, "SHIT" is hard to reproduce accurately; yet Sophia managed it with perfect diction one day when she spilled cranberry juice all over the blue living room rug—her utterance pre-empting my own. And I felt assured of Sophia's linguistic competence the day that, upon my yelling "Oh God!" (as I watched a bowl of chocolate pudding splatter the kitchen wall), Sophia exclaimed "Jesus!" with just the right intonation.

Galicia, 1876

IF PEARL CAN BE SURE OF ANYTHING, *it is that God— blessed be He—works in mysterious ways.*

Swathed by the girls in the day, Pearl is caught off guard when Moshe comes to her bed one night. His body feels heavy and his mouth is rough. He touches her hair, searches her face. His eyes beg her to see him but Pearl is unsure if she wants to look. Maybe it's better that they cannot read each other's faces. As she feels him enter her, she blurts out her fears. He wraps his arms around her, whispers words of faith. Words she is not sure either of them believe.

Night after night, Moshe reaches for her. Within a few months, she knows she has conceived again. Her breasts swell, her belly rounds. Everywhere Pearl goes, people talk and she bristles. "May this one be a boy, yes? A hearing boy!" No matter that Nellie and Bayla are standing right by her side, reading their lips, their faces. Pearl begins to stay at home, keeping the girls there with her whenever she can. When Nellie and Bayla get restless, she sends them outside. At five and three, they chase the chickens or pet the goats in the shade of a tree.

Late one afternoon, Pearl stands in the open doorway, the dusky air a relief from the heat of the day. She breathes in the scents of wood, apricot, and straw. A shriek jolts Pearl's body a few steps out the door. A rock flies past her in the direction of the ridge, its arc cutting the thick air. Then another rock, aired from the opposite direction. A volley of thuds, then high-pitched yowlings, like pained cats. "Where? Where are you? Nellie!" Pearl chastises herself as she runs: she shouldn't have let the girls alone, she should have been watching them. The rocks are still flying, one landing now near her foot. Pearl tops the hill, and sees five or six boys scattering. She strains to recognize them—are they the peasant boys who sell grain at the market?

A soft whimper forces her eyes away from the boys to a clutched heap just steps away from her now. Her girls lie in the grass, their arms bent over their heads, their fingers intertwined. So many rocks, aimed at their ears. They yelp violently when Pearl first kneels down to comfort them, then they bury their streaming faces in the folds of her skirts.

Pearl lifts her daughters and carries them crumpled, one in each arm, over the hill and into the house. She slams the door behind her with new fear, new hatred. She couldn't be sure those boys were from the market, the ones she saw running away. Who, then? As she cleans her girls' scrapes, dries their blood, she vows to help them. She speaks to them now in a steady stream and they watch her through their tears. For a long while, they lie folded in her embrace.

That night, Pearl feeds Moshe dinner, then sits him in the living room chair.

"I could kill those boys." Pearl waits for her bottom lip to stop trembling. "There is a young woman, Rayzl. Chava told me about her—they met at the book bazaar. Her parents are deaf and so are several of her aunts. She used a hand language before she learned to speak. Moshe—maybe she can tutor the girls, help them. Who knows, maybe she can teach them to speak? She was just married. Why don't you go talk to her husband. I can scrimp at the market to pay for lessons—please, Moshe."

Moshe considers this, then stands up. From the bedroom doorway, he looks in on Nellie and Bayla as they sleep. Even in the darkness, he can see that Nellie's lips are dark red and swollen. Bayla's arms are cut and bruised. How could this happen?

Moshe pulls at his shirtsleeves, cuffing them close around his wrists. "All right, Pearl," he mutters. "I will go."

◆ ◆ ◆

The morning Rayzl begins her tutelage, Nellie and Bayla start out shyly, knitted close to Pearl's sides. But as Rayzl gestures broadly to them, her face open and warm, the girls sidle nearer.

Pearl watches her girls fluttering around their new teacher, and now unexpectedly she aches with regret. Jealousy. She should be teaching them about the world all around. She should know them—their thoughts, their fears, their wishes and dreams. Yet she does not. Not in their intricacies. Nellie and Bayla have grown together, bonded in their deafness, as if inside an unbroken circle. For someone else now—a stranger— to weave herself in! It's what Pearl wanted for them, yes, so that they could learn and grow stronger. And yet . . .

Rayzl walks through the village with Nellie and Bayla at her sides. She stops often to point at a familiar object. Then she signs its name. Inside the bakery: the mandel bread, the almond cakes, the babkes, the rugelach. Along the river path: the oaks and lindens, the grey mushrooms, the blackberry vines. At the market: the meats and fish, the buckwheat groats, the spices, the vinegars, the salves, the leathers. And hooked under everyone's arm, the baskets for toting their finds and trades. Back at home: the tables and chairs, the beds and trunks, the books, the yarns, the Shabbat candles and candlesticks. In an excited daze, Nellie imitates Rayzl's signs. She shows Rayzl their own homemade signs for things, some so alike; some so different from hers. With each new name she learns from Rayzl, Nellie beams as if she has acquired the thing itself.

Week after week, Nellie's dictionary, and her universe, grows. "Apricot is rock," Nellie signs at lunchtime, to convey her fruit's hardness. Now Rayzl works, not just on the names of objects, but on descriptors, the qualities of things. The wax is hot; the bucket is empty; the table is thick; the wild strawberries are sweet. Bayla does not advance so quickly. She often breaks away in the middle of a lesson, settling herself in the barn until Nellie retrieves her.

Most nights before bed, Nellie carries the oil lamp to her bedside, and she practices flattening, rounding, blowing, popping, and puffing her mouth the way Rayzl has showed her. On the eve of her seventh birthday, Nellie stares into the small, smoky looking-glass and studies her face—her eyes, the bridge of her nose, the angle of her cheeks, her ears. Her worthless ears. Nellie lowers the mirror slightly to her lips, and looks on as the pout in her lips becomes a sputter, itchy and tickly at the same time. Her new baby sister, Elish, laughs to see Nellie's faces. Nellie cheers a little, and uses the mirror to play peek-a-boo.

◆ ◆ ◆

Chava, who knew Rayzl first, stops often at the house, delighting the girls with honey cakes and scraps of bright colored cloth for dressing up their ragdolls. She sits with Pearl over sweet mint tea while Rayzl tutors Nellie and Bayla, and together they wonder at Rayzl's magic.

When in summer Chava takes to bed in a difficult pregnancy, Nellie and Bayla visit her at her bedside, giving her their quiet company. One day, Chava's elderly mother shoos them away at the door with a despairing look in her eye. Nellie and Bayla turn from the door, confused. Then they see something trailing out of Chava's bedroom window. A string, beginning with a loop from Chava's bedpost, crisscrosses Tasse like a Cat's Cradle. Nellie and Bayla follow the string this way and that through the village, until they come to the synagogue. The string is a prayer made visible, looped by Chava's husband from home to the Ark. Now, he is crumpled in prayer, crying before the Holy Scrolls for the safety of Chava and their not-yet-born baby.

Nellie and Bayla sit gravely on a bench outside the sanctuary, until Moshe spots their dusky shadows and leads them home. In the middle of the night, Pearl shakes them awake. Nellie rushes to the front door and there she sees a length of string trailing low along the ground, caked in dirt. Whimpers of grief clump and fall like wet snowflakes from Chava's bedroom window. Sorrow, no less felt when unheard.

Massachusetts, December 2002

WE TIED A STRING BETWEEN Sophia's hearing aids to hold them in place in her ears, and to keep them from getting lost when they came out. The audiologist provided it: a bright yellow string, threaded into a perfect child-sized clip. My hands shook the first time I looped up Sophia's hearing aids to the yellow line and attached the clip to the back of her t-shirt. There were strings *everywhere*—my thoughts, their own tangled Cat's Cradle; my feelings of grief, never far away.

One day, in the supermarket, the yellow string caught the attention of a little boy. Sophia was sitting in our shopping cart, holding her favorite blanket. The boy walked up to Sophia, and stared at the bright string and at the hearing aids it linked. Wordlessly, he reached up and yanked at the string, causing one hearing aid to pop out of Sophia's ear.

"No, boy!" Sophia said, wagging her finger. She was nearly two and a half years old.

I looked into the boy's face, trying to distinguish whether his act was borne of curiosity, or of malice, or some combination of the two. I decided on curiosity. So, I explained, "You know how some people wear glasses to help them see better? Well, my little girl, Sophia, wears hearing aids to help her hear better. This yellow string keeps her hearing aids in place." I spoke in my most matter-of-fact voice, as I put Sophia's hearing aid back into her ear.

"Oh," the little boy said, watching intently. A woman's call of "Timothy, Timothy!" caused him to turn and wander away.

As Sophia and I walked on, she said, "I hear with my hearin' aids."

"That's right, honey," I answered.

Then, noticing the rows of food around her, Sophia shouted, "Pasta!"

"Yes, that's the kind you like."

"Pickles!"

"Yes, honey."

I steered Sophia into the next aisle. Right in front of us stood Jan.

"Hey! How are you two?" Jan asked, and gave us each a hug.

I started to blurt out what just happened with the little boy, but Sophia interrupted.

"Jan, I really non't like wasabi."

"Oh?"

Then Sophia said thoughtfully, about her pediatrician, "Dr. Kenny smells like peaches."

Jan and I burst out laughing.

"To answer your question, Jan, we're fine," I said. "We're just fine."

◆ ◆ ◆

Bill and I spoke of having another baby. We didn't speak openly about the possibility of a second baby's deafness. At a genetics consult shortly after Sophia's birth, we were given a lab requisition form to test for genetic deafness. We never used it. The tests had to be run on Sophia's blood—a lot of it—and we didn't want to stress her tiny body for the sake of our knowledge base. The only other test our insurance company would cover was a test of my amniotic fluid when a fetus was already in utero. We had my father's fax, of course, which seemed proof enough that I, at least, contributed a genetic deafness component. No one in Bill's family had a record or even a recollection of deaf relatives. Still, it seemed likely—even if wildly coincidental—that Bill and I were both recessive gene carriers. How else to explain the fact that Bill and I were hearing, while Sophia was not? It couldn't be a dominant gene just from me, because a dominant gene would have rendered me hearing impaired, too. Under the recessive gene theory, there was a 25 percent chance that our next baby would have hearing loss, too. It was not a negligible chance.

My mind spun with thoughts of deaf siblings—of Nellie and Bayla, as I'd been imagining them: at the river, their toes grabbing the mushy bottom; at the market, their noses filled with the sharp smells of vinegar and fish; upon the shul bench, their eyes glued to the sanctuary door, to the crisscrossed length of string leading to the men's gallery. All the accompanying sounds naturally arising in my mind, muted out. My ancestors' existences, shrouded in silence and isolation.

Yet when I focused my attention on Sophia, I saw my self-possessed little girl engaged with family and friends. Turning to voices. Chattering away. Not just in English, either; during Hanukkah, Sophia imitated the Hebrew words we sang as we lit our menorah! We had so many advantages—education and resources and technology. We felt equipped to deal with hearing loss. The risk that our next baby would be hearing impaired wasn't so worrying. We were buoyed by Sophia's wellness.

◆ ◆ ◆

Each morning, when the *New York Times* arrived at our doorstep, Sophia would toddle down the front steps to get it while Bill stood propped in the doorway, ready to catch its inner sections as Sophia bustled her way back inside. One September morning, Sophia paused as she leaned over the paper, its top half spread flat upon our brick walkway. There was a picture of a firefighter kneeling in solemn grief at a 9/11 memorial site. Without a word, Sophia gathered up the paper in her arms. She walked past Bill and went inside, took a Band Aid from the low kitchen cabinet, and placed it on the firefighter.

Sophia's word list, still on our refrigerator, now included not just "happy" and "sad" but "excited," "disappointed," "worried," "scared," and "silly." Sophia was particularly attuned to facial expressions, and at two plus years old, feelings were her focus. When one day I praised her for being generous to another toddler, she said, "I am generous, but I also have jealous." And when I offered to make a face out of whipped cream for her dessert, she requested a face that was "frustrated."

Sophia was oblivious to most social niceties. One night, at a neighborhood diner in time to catch the "early bird special," Sophia pointed both at the leftover cups of coffee and at the predominantly elderly eaters and shouted:

"OLD, OLD, OLD!" We thought this was typical two-year-old fare, and (while horrified) we reveled in the normality of it. But when I told Jan, she said, "That's such a "deaf" thing!" Are the deaf just naturally and excruciatingly direct? In the Signing community, they certainly don't pull any punches—just look up the sign for "fat" and you'll see.

Sophia began to converse, even bicker, with her best friend, Ben. They bickered mainly over the sippy cup of water that Sophia offered to Ben again and again, despite his patient declining and then his adamant refusals. It was a thrill to hear them in dialogue, in toddler-speak. Sophia delighted in choosing the colors of her newest set of earmolds: bright blues, pinks, purples, and greens swirled together. And at a birthday party for a friend, she sang "Happy Birthday," enunciating the lyrics perfectly in full voice and astonishingly right on pitch. I looked across the room at Bill, whose eyes were welled up with tears. Neither one of us could have hoped for better. So many gains; at two and a half, Sophia's language and speech were at her peer level.

Only her weight trailed behind. We soldiered on with pasta and cream.

◆ ◆ ◆

To celebrate an anniversary, we arranged for Sophia to stay home with a trusted babysitter, and Bill and I went for a night away at a nearby inn. The next morning, we stopped at a bakery for pastries. A petite, elderly woman toting a big suitcase stopped us to ask for directions to a local shrine. When we got our bearings in the small Berkshire town, and realized that her destination was up a steep, winding road, Bill offered to drive her there.

On the windy hilltop at Marian Fathers Mercy Monastery, the lady took our hands in hers. *"You will have many blessings,"* she said. She stood stalwart in the gusts, waving until we drove out of sight. I couldn't know then that one was already burrowing in my womb. We would name her Juliet.

◆ ◆ ◆

At first, I was ill in the usual ways of pregnancy. Then I became ill in unusual ways. Shingles. Thyroid problems. A raging breast infection. The doctors couldn't say what caused the infection—perhaps a remnant of the mastitis I'd had while nursing Sophia, breeding now at pregnancy speed.

Seven months into the pregnancy, I lay in bed, listless and disoriented. The peach paint on our bedroom walls, a once cheerily soothing palette of historical colors, closed in on me: I had the not-so-fleeting thought that I was going to be smothered by someone in a flesh-colored leotard. I was home from Mass General Hospital after a surgery to remove the infectious tissue, but the infection was up and raging again. I was taking an IV dose of antibiotics and had a huge hole in my breast. When I looked down into it, I felt unsteady and faint. Visiting nurses came twice a day to pack and unpack it, and I had been instructed to shower four times a day, to let the hottest water I could bear run into it.

Before the surgery, I had let Sophia climb into bed with me while I rested. There was a novelty, then, to my being home in bed in the middle of the day, and I could still manage to be upbeat. One afternoon, as Sophia wriggled her feet under my white down comforter, she brushed her bare toes against my legs. "Mama, you're wearing new pants." By toes alone, she learned that I had transitioned to the next stage in maternity clothes.

Once the nurses started coming, Bill and I arranged a schedule so that Sophia was shielded from all of it—a schedule that took Bill away too, and I was left largely alone and lonely. Too hot and loopy to concentrate on anything, my consolation and my company was the baby inside me—my Juliet, though I didn't know her yet—and Lucca, who sat at the side of the bed, protecting me, barking at the nurses, nuzzling me when they came near. Lucca was sick, too, with inoperable cancer in her bladder. We had discovered it months ago, when she began peeing bright red blood into spring's green grass. In a sunny spot in my bedroom, Lucca's wide eyes betrayed her discomfort as she shifted positions, circling again and again before gingerly sitting herself down. Once down, she panted heavily, her black lips wide open like the Joker of *Batman* days. I dangled my arm off the bed, stretching my fingers to caress her soft, felted ears.

Lying in bed, I was pumped up with countless hard-hitting antibiotics, the dosages of which, I'd ascertained from obsessive online searches, had never been tested on humans. Only mice, and not even pregnant ones. My OB scheduled extra sonograms with the intent to reassure me, but each one showed a fetus moving very little or not at all. The technicians suggested it was natural for the baby to be "quiet," given all that I was going through.

A chunk of my breast missing. What might be missing in my baby? My worries for Juliet were unspeakable.

Massachusetts, September 2003

SOPHIA CAME IN for good-night snuggles. I held her tight against my huge belly. Her brown hair was growing long, her bangs feathering out around her wide eyes. I wondered how she felt about this impending baby, her big sister-hood bought, these past months, at a higher-than-usual price. The possibility of the baby's deafness—how might it affect their relationship? Would they share a universe, their breaths, their thoughts, even their dreams, synchronized?

Did I *expect* the new baby to be deaf? Did I *hope* it, for Sophia's sake, supposing that it might be easier if her sibling was deaf? My speech had become so exaggeratedly precise and loud. Would I even know how to talk to a hear-ing newborn, in soft whispers and coos? *Could I admit to myself that I longed for my new baby to hear?*

At this point, deafness was the least of our worries. With all that was going wrong, I didn't know what to expect, or what to hope for. I could hardly find my hopes amidst my fears for this child. At night, in bed, I searched Bill's face. He looked back at me, blankly. Perhaps Bill had tucked away his hopes, too. I rolled over to sleep. My journal lay, bound and untouched, in my dresser drawer.

Weeks passed and the infection continued to rage. Our faith in the Mass General surgeon faded. My father researched and arranged an appointment with another surgeon reputed to be one of the best in New York City. One hot, sticky morning, early in my ninth month of pregnancy, I hugged Bill and Sophia and boarded an Amtrak train to Penn Station. My sister met me there, held my hand, took me to meet the surgeon, then to her apartment on West Eighty-third Street.

My sister and I had become close in college. She'd transferred to Barnard, up by Columbia, and we lived just across Broadway from each other. We met for dinner at least once a week back then, usually at the Hungarian restaurant for chicken paprikash. We studied together in her dorm room, went shopping, talked constantly on the phone. Years later, she would give Lucca to us after spotting her in an abandoned Brooklyn parking lot and nursing her back to health. I was sorry that my sister and I hadn't been closer as children—that it took leaving home for us to open up to each other.

In my sister's apartment, decorated in "retro" style with

my grandmother's ornate furniture, I lay ill in her bed, propped up by fluffy pillows and eating comfort food she'd ordered in from a local diner—matzoh brie and rugelach. I spoke to Bill and Sophia by phone. The next morning, my mother met me at the surgery center on the Upper East Side.

The second surgery left me scarred and bereft of one-third of my breast tissue but, finally, infection-free. When I returned home, Bill made me tea and situated me in bed. Sophia fussed over me, stroking my head, asking if she could kiss my "line" to make me all better. Lucca circled the bed, barking out her welcome.

When my labor began a few weeks later, Bill called the babysitter to come stay with Sophia and Lucca. As we waited, Sophia watched me curiously. I tried to conceal the pain of the contractions coming every five minutes. I turned my face away, bending my body this way and that. At one point I hunched over a plant and pretended to check its soil while my uterus squeezed and cramped. Bill and I reached the labor and delivery unit when I was six centimeters dilated and in active labor. In less than an hour, I was nine centimeters dilated.

Then, my labor stalled. For the next eight hours, I labored in excruciating pain, with no advancement. Of the five doctors in my OB practice, the youngest and least experienced was on call at the hospital that day. She came into our labor room in the midst of it and sat herself down in a rocking chair. She wore bright red clogs with her hospital scrubs, and she just sat, rocking, while I labored. Bill held onto me as I worked with birthing balls and squatting bars. The doctor prattled on about the Red Sox game and other things. Could I ask her to leave? I tried to keep my focus on birthing. She continued her chitchatting. Finally, she went on her rounds.

Moments after the doctor left the room, I started to push out Juliet. A nurse called her back, handing her a box of sterile gloves. The doctor warned me that I was not yet at the pushing stage. But the raw, gripping insistence of my body won out. Despite all of the anti-infection drugs, the general anesthesia during my breast surgeries, and the worries about low fetal movement, Juliet was born perfectly, beautifully—*blessedly*—intact.

I woke to see a hospital nurse standing over Juliet, and in a surge of panic I attempted a sit-up. My womb paid me back with a clotty gush of blood, my abdomen with a deep crampy pain. Chastened, I twisted and wiggled myself gently to a seated position, put on my glasses, then demanded to know what was happening. I saw that Juliet was swaddled and sleeping, but with electrodes stuck to her head and blue gooey stuff oozing into her hairline. Before the nurse could explain, I reminded her that I gave explicit instructions that Bill or I be awake and present for any tests they run, especially the hearing screen.

The nurse gave me a measured look and said, "I am just repeating the hearing test to be sure of the result."

"*Repeating?*"

"Yes. Your husband was with me yesterday when I performed it the first time. You were sleeping." The white drawstring on her hospital pants had the blue goo on it, too.

Flushing hot, I propped a pillow behind me and leaned back against its cool side. Bill was here this morning. He didn't tell me. "She failed it?"

"Yes. But I thought I'd run it once more to be sure."

The crampy pain was back and I shifted positions. "Is she failing it now?"

"Yes."

At home, I laid Juliet down on a satin-edged baby blanket in the center of the living room floor. The smell of her diaper cream mingled with our wool rug, rough beneath my knees. My breasts ached under the medical order not to breastfeed Juliet in the wake of the surgeries. Cabbage leaves and frozen peas, fabled to quell lactation, rustled inside my bra.

I tried to meet Juliet's gaze, but her eyes didn't register mine. She looked in my direction, but past me, through me, toward the sunlit window. It struck me that she had not yet met my gaze. I leaned over her, positioning my face directly in front of hers, but she still didn't look at me. She began to arch her back. Little scales of cradle cap flecked from her scalp and floated in the air.

Juliet's spine formed a perfect bridge, her weight balanced on the soft spot of her head. I rearranged her, bending her knees up toward her belly to force a concave posture, but as soon as I took my hands off of her, she reassumed the arch position. I backed away from her—was she arching to get distance from me?—but she stayed in her backbend, the light from the window bouncing off of her upside-down chin.

My baby couldn't hear me. And she wasn't looking at me, either. Whatever competence I felt as a mother the second time around—I was skilled now at newborn feeding and diapering and bathing and swaddling—was undermined by Juliet's inexplicable arching, by her distant gaze, by the unknown degree of her hearing loss.

I went into the kitchen to make a bottle. As with Sophia during those first weeks, every sound was exaggerated for me now that I knew Juliet was probably unable to hear it: the faucet rush of water, the scooping of the formula powder, the shaking of the mixture—I could make this louder or softer depending on how vigorously I shook—then the second faucet rush of water to heat the bottle. Finally, the sound of the canister rotating on the countertop; I turned it so I didn't have to see the mocking words "Breast milk is best . . ." as I walked back to the living room.

In the living room, Juliet was still arched back. I scooped her up, but like a fish, she flipped and flailed. I nestled her into the crook of my arm and placed the bottle to her lips, but she squirmed herself to an upright sitting position with her back to me. She wanted to face out as she drank her bottle, her eyes away from me.

How were we going to relate to each other? All my worries about motherhood were back, strong as ever. With Juliet here, I'd be less available for Sophia. Juggling two, I'd be less focused than with one. And my girls' deafness, on top of everything, was like an enduring signpost of my *own* impediments to hearing, to connection and closeness.

I draped Juliet over my shoulder to burp her, and sang to her from a mixed-up, past repertoire of show tunes and operatic arias. I landed on a song I remembered all the words to,

Freddie's song from *My Fair Lady*. I could picture the freck-led, redheaded boy who sang the song in the production I was in as a teenager, when I dreamed of becoming a singer. *"I have often walked down this street before. But the pavement always stayed beneath my feet before. All at once am I several stories high, knowing I'm on the street where you live."* The boy belted it out and now so did I. I didn't stop for Bill's foot-steps down the stairs, and I continued on as he watched.

"I don't think she can hear anything at all," Bill said when I was finished. The brainstem test that would tell the exact degree of Juliet's hearing loss was a week away, but Bill repeatedly expressed his impression that Juliet was completely deaf. He paired himself with Sophia—whom I now missed desperately—while I, exclusively, cared for Juliet. I thought back to how Bill had held Sophia as a new-born, how he had balanced her in her entirety upon his strong forearm, zooming her face close to mine for kisses, then swaying her gently to sleep. Was it just the logistics of a second baby—a natural, sensible division of labor—that split us so? Or had the prospect of complete deafness driven Bill away?

"She can hear my singing," I said assuredly, and I moved on to "Quando Men Vo" from *La Boheme*.

But in the middle I stopped. Bill was in the kitchen and I asked him to come back.

"What about her sight, Bill? Do you think she can see?"

"I am not sure," he said, his eyes not meeting mine now either.

◆ ◆ ◆

Surrounded by old people wearing flimsy grey goggles, I sat with Juliet at the ophthalmologist's office and narrated board books. *The Three Bears. Hop on Pop. Time for Bed.* When I came to *Brown Bear Brown Bear, What Do You See?* hastily stuffed into the diaper bag, I cast it aside and then thrust all the books back into the bag. It was doubtful that Juliet could hear anything I was saying to her, and with tears flooding my eyes and occluding my own vision, I was panicked that she couldn't see. I sat impatiently, holding Juliet face-out as was usual now, and racked my brain for the information I once knew about Usher's Disease, the syndrome in which deafness is linked with blindness.

The waiting was interminable. The room smelled like formaldehyde mixed with ammonia. We were taken in for dilating drops, then sent back into the crowded waiting room. *Highlights. Your Big Backyard.* I couldn't just sit there without showing her anything. When we were finally taken in to meet with the doctor, Juliet was squirmy from having sat so long. Quickly, the doctor shined a light into the backs of her eyes to examine her pupils. Just as he lowered the light, Juliet looked into my eyes for the first time. She looked into my eyes! I grabbed Juliet close in the darkness, and between heaving breaths, I planted soft kisses all over her face—her cheeks, her lips, her nose, and her eyes—her sparkling, light-filled, blueberry eyes.

◆ ◆ ◆

Just weeks after Juliet's arrival, I was preparing to teach again at Mount Holyoke College. Thankfully, I was slated to teach just one class: Introduction to Philosophy.

I knew better than to lead off with Bishop Berkeley. But there I was, standing at the blackboard, launching into idealism. I could see from the telltale signs of shifting and fidgeting that my students' minds were beginning to wander. Just a few more words about Berkeley's main tenet—to be is to be perceived—and my mind wandered, too.

I couldn't shake a dream I had had the previous night. A lone girl was standing at the edge of a large field. Wild gusts of freezing air swept through the landscape and the ground froze in an instant. The girl fell upon the cold earth, blades of brittle grass snapping beneath her. She cupped her frost-bitten hands to her ears, as the lullabies that welled inside her memory went silent. Just when she began to shriek, I woke in a clammy sweat. Juliet was crying.

As I stood before my class, I watched the chalk dust drift soundlessly onto the sill and I wondered: Did anyone ever perceive my mother? Did anyone perceive Nellie or Bayla? Did Pearl?

Just days ago, I had received an e-mail message from my cousin Valerie. She still hadn't been able to locate Bayla or Pearl in any available US Census Reports. Maybe they never got to the US, or maybe they changed their names at the gateway. That same day I received a CD Valerie prepared for me, with a picture of Pearl burned onto it. I viewed Pearl on my computer screen. Strength emanated from the sharp curve of her brow, the jut of her chin. Her dark irises settled in on me, bobbing in large pools of white. Eyes, I imagined, that wouldn't hastily turn away.

Still at the blackboard, goose-fleshed now with white powder dusting my arms and flecking my black pants, I feared for Sophia and Juliet. For me. How could *I* reflect back their existence, their meaning? I, who was more transparent than chalk dust, a child who grew up on the edge of a home before eyes that turned inevitably inward, unable to mark me in a spot for real.

Massachusetts, October 2003

THE DAY JULIET TURNED SIX WEEKS OLD, we headed to the audiology clinic at Boston Children's Hospital. Sophia would spend the morning playing with her friend Ben. I climbed into the back of the car beside Juliet, with the diaper bag full of bottles, board books, finger puppets and rattles. I would entertain her for the two hours while Bill drove.

I was still always paired with Juliet. Bill was slow to bond with her, and I took it personally. After the tumult of this pregnancy and Juliet's vision scare, I was wholly identified with her. Why wasn't he enamored with her, like I was? I felt rejected on Juliet's behalf.

The few times I spoke to Bill about it, he shrugged it off, saying everything would be fine. Bill had a faith in us, even in our disconnections and absences, that I couldn't fathom. The slightest shake up and I imagined devastation at our roots. But Bill kept his gaze fixed on our foundations: we were solid and strong, our love for each other thick and true. His faith didn't always translate into closeness, though. Steady and sure could be far away, remote.

In the car, I focused my attention on Juliet. I fit a sleek purple butterfly puppet on my finger, then made it flutter around the back seat before landing with a tickle and a kiss upon Juliet's cheek. Flutter, tickle kiss. Flutter, tickle kiss. Juliet's squeals and laughter filled my ears until the moment we entered the sound booth to discover the degree of her deafness.

"Profound." According to the audiologist, Juliet could not hear anything—not a running lawn mower, not a revving jet engine. Most likely, the thousands of tiny hairs, the cilia, that normally line the inner ear and stimulate the auditory nerve, were in Juliet's case broken, bent, or missing. Hearing aids, even the most powerful ones, wouldn't enable her to hear spoken language.

Bill and I didn't speak. I crossed the room to where Juliet lay asleep on the examination table. I picked her up and held her tight to my chest.

The audiologist suggested we schedule another test that would tell us exactly *how* profound Juliet's hearing loss was. I wondered why we should bother. Did it really matter where, in the range of profound deafness, Juliet's hearing loss lay? I resisted, on the grounds that another sedation would leave Juliet either inconsolably cranky or vomiting as she was earlier today. But my resistance was to the news itself. I was used to hearing impairment but not stone deafness.

◆ ◆ ◆

On the drive home, Juliet slept. After an hour in the car, silent, I looked through the materials the audiologist had handed us: information about cochlear implants, a surgical technology that could possibly give Juliet access to sound; pamphlets on sign language classes; the names of websites, of parents, of schools, both oral and manual. Here we were again, at the center of the Oral/Deaf divide. But this time, with the diagnosis of *profound* deafness, we couldn't be sure that the oral approach was even an option. Juliet would need an MRI first, to determine if her cochlea was structurally intact for an implant. She couldn't get that test until she was six months old. The implant surgery itself couldn't be scheduled before her first birthday—the FDA doesn't approve of it earlier—and then, who knew whether it would enable her, successfully, to hear and to speak?

If an oral framework turned out to be impossible for Juliet, how would we manage as a family? How were we to forge bonds with our baby? How would our extended families and our friends ever get to know Juliet?

There wasn't a large Deaf community in Northampton. Even if *we* gained fluency in Sign, Juliet would be isolated here. We would have to relocate to somewhere with a large Deaf community so that she could make Deaf friends, have Deaf teachers, Deaf role models.

I knew firsthand the challenges of learning Sign. Despite consistent efforts, I still had a limited grasp of its grammar. But I was determined to learn it now, while we figured out our options.

I fished out my cell phone and dialed the number on the "Family Sign Language Program" pamphlet. In a faltering voice, I explained that we had a profoundly deaf baby. We knew some signs, but not sign language, and we needed to learn. They arranged for a teacher to come to our house that weekend.

A woman with short black hair and a narrow, ruddy face arrived at our door on Saturday morning. Her name was Cynthia. She waved hello and walked into the house. Bill carried Sophia down the stairs, still in her pajamas. I cradled Juliet in my arms. We stood awkwardly in the entryway for several minutes.

The person on the phone had said that the Deaf teacher

would be joined by an interpreter. The interpreter was late. Despite the Sign vocabulary I'd amassed, I was practically non-conversant. I motioned to the couch, and we all sat, waiting.

The minutes ticked by. Cynthia smiled at Sophia, motioning for her to come closer. I pantomimed the offer of hot tea, which luckily Cynthia accepted. The relief of heading into the kitchen for the kettle mutated into worry as I walked back into the living room with the mugs. How was I going to communicate with this woman? How was I going to learn from her what I needed, in order to communicate with Juliet?

The interpreter knocked just then, and for the next hour, she translated back and forth as Cynthia set a schedule for the next ten weeks. She explained that there would be no interpreter after this first meeting; we'd have to get along in Sign.

The following Saturday we began again, sitting awkwardly on the living room couch. Cynthia signed and we watched. We imitated her hands, uncertainly. She pointed to our expressionless faces, then she modeled expressiveness: eyebrows furrowed for questioning, cheeks buoyed for excitement, mouth and eyes scowling for anger, shoulders drooped for disappointment, and so on. It wasn't just our hands we'd have to train.

Juliet still arched backwards, despite our constant efforts to reposition her. Our audiologist wondered if she was trying to see behind herself. Juliet was doggedly persistent, undeterred, not to be redirected. We gave her a Sign name like a boomerang, formed with the hand shaped into the letter J, swooping out from her heart and landing back where it started. Sophia chose her own Sign name: her hand shaped into the letter S, moving in the arc of a rainbow.

Week after week, I faltered but managed to learn some Sign. Bill sat through the weekly sessions barely moving. He told me his hands were not dexterous. I gave him sign language flashcards and a computer CD. I begged him to practice.

At some point Bill's hands became cracked and torn, and no amount of lotion, cream, or even prescribed medicine could heal them. It may have been the bottle washing, compounded by the New England dryness. Or it may have been my anger—at the way his hands weren't signing with Juliet—that had its way with them.

For the next few months, I cornered the deaf people I met, strangers in the street, and I asked for the chance to try to sign with them. In the house, I signed alone, bitter at Bill for not trying harder, fearful that Juliet would not see a whole language if I was the only one using it.

Whatever I had thought about our family being equipped to handle deafness was *all wrong*. At night, I began writing again—I hadn't been able to write since before the breast surgeries and Juliet's birth—and now I could see my fear and anger steering my stories. I imagined Nellie and Bayla entirely shut out from family conversations. Moshe's ponderous utterances reeled out invisibly from his lips, obscured by his beard. When he pounded the table with dramatic flourish, the girls startled and shook. In my imagining, he never learned a single one of their signs. I wouldn't let him.

During the day, I researched cochlear implants. Bill and I spoke to parents, audiologists, and teachers. We read articles and met with doctors. We scheduled the MRI and other preliminary tests. If Juliet was a candidate, the surgery could take place in September—seven silent, languageless months from now. Bill and I argued over the fact of his not signing.

"Jennifer, I am just not good at signing."

"You need to *practice*. What if she's not a candidate for the implant? Or what if it's not successful? We need a language with her."

"Then I'll work at it."

"Even if she *can* get the implant, don't you want to be able to talk to her when it's off: at bedtime, in the bath? In the middle of the night, when she wakes up from a dream, don't you want her to be able to describe it to you, and not wait and forget her dream by morning?"

More than anything, I wanted our family to embrace this language now, this language that required us to stay present to each other, to not turn away. A bridge to the silent world. How could I make him understand?

My eyes blurry with tears, I looked across the room at Juliet. She was lying back on a blanket, her hands up close to her face. I wiped my eyes to see her better. Her fingers were weaving patterns in the air—threads of Sign. Juliet was babbling with her hands!

At five months old, Juliet was signing words. A pulsating fist for milk. A knock in the air for yes. A finger peck to the thumb for chicken. Light on; duck; book; water; shoes. Sophia was signing too, and she was the first to notice when Juliet picked up a new sign. "Mama, Juliet is making the sign for cheese!" I looked at Juliet's hands and saw that she had put the heels of her palms together and was making a twisting gesture: cheese.

◆ ◆ ◆

When I sat, holding Juliet, Sophia wedged her way onto my lap. "Let me in!" she'd say, and I'd wiggle and rearrange

Juliet to make room for Sophia. Then Sophia would pet Juliet on her fuzzy head, and say in baby talk, "Are you hungry, honey? Want a bottle?" Or she'd pick up a familiar book and recite it to Juliet from memory. "Chrysanthemum didn't *think* her name was perfect, She *knew* it." Other times, Sophia would act out her displacement, fretting and whacking her doll against the wood edge of the windowseat. At still other times, Sophia would look into my eyes and say, "Right now, I wish it were just you, me, and daddy." Often, I'd hug her tightly and say, "I understand how you feel, Sophia," swallowing my fears that Sophia and Juliet might not grow close.

But there were times when I'd lose my composure and resent Sophia's rejection of Juliet. "She's part of our family, Soph," I'd bark, full of intolerance. I'd find myself making demands on Sophia, demands too big for a three year old: "You'll just have to wait," or "Go look at books by yourself until I'm ready," or "You are a big girl now—you're crying over *this?*" I'd speak in a harsh tone, the displeasure in my face seeping into her skin. What scared me the most was how erratic I could be—full of sweet patience and generosity one minute, a biting sharpness the next. Shuddering, I'd rehearse consistent, empathetic responses: "This must be hard for you," or "It's frustrating, isn't it, to have to wait," or "I see how sad you feel."

I treated the girls differently, despite myself. Partly because Juliet was just a baby, and she was my second, I found her easier to handle. If she turned over the cereal box, I'd see it as developmental: "she's dumping." If Sophia did it, I'd see it as an awful mess, one I didn't need on top of everything else. I apologized to Sophia. But even if she could forgive me, I found it difficult to forgive myself.

◆ ◆ ◆

Around the time Juliet was six months old, we were invited to a children's music concert. A friend was playing a guitar part, so even though Juliet wouldn't be able to hear it, we decided to go. Sophia stood at the edge of the stage with her friends, Ben and Katie, and danced. Bill and I sat in chairs. I held Juliet in my lap, bouncing her to the beat of the music. Juliet seemed bored and tired. Then, suddenly, she wriggled out of my grip, maneuvered off my lap and laid herself flat on the concrete floor by my feet. She pressed her whole body and the side of her face against the cold, dirty, concrete floor. A few minutes later she jerked up to her knees, turned to face us, and smiled broadly before flopping back down. She felt the whole concert from down on the floor.

Afterwards, we bought the concert CD, and for the

first time since we swayed to foreign lullabies with Sophia cradled in our arms, we played music in our house. Bill and I took turns swinging Sophia around and then Juliet. From "Possum in the Kitchen," we switched to other CDs. We listened to old songs—"Locomotion"—and songs from our courtship—"Every Little Kiss" and "How Sweet It Is To Be Loved By You." Lucca barked excitedly, her tail and even her low hips swaying to the rhythm of "Brown Eyed Girl."

We had stopped listening to music because background sound of any kind interfered with Sophia's access to language. But now Sophia's language pickup was unstoppable, and music could be added into the auditory mix. Sophia herself asked for "lassical" music. When Bill put on Handel's *Messiah*, Sophia sat on the couch and attentively listened to it.

I hadn't realized my own deprivation until the loss was restored. Now I wanted to blare music at top volume: "C'MON BABY DRIVE SOUTH. WITH THE ONE YOU LOVE." I wanted it to reverberate in my body like an electrical current. Of course, this caused Juliet to jump three feet off the floor because of the vibrations. So I held her up, way up in my arms, and she felt the music off the floor, up high in my pounding, pumped up, drowned out heart.

◆ ◆ ◆

I found a new kind of trust after that concert. Juliet was flourishing; she was developing and learning through all her other senses. She alerted to our footfall and expected us at her bedroom door from the vibrations of our steps. She received my songs, even without hearing a sound, when I sang with her draped across my chest. Sophia, too, was compensating for her hearing loss in incredible ways, through sight and smell. Do hearing children know who stopped by the house while they were out, just by olfactory cues? Sophia could smell who came over while she was off at school! We hesitated to tell this to people, because it made them feel smelly.

I used to puzzle, as a philosopher, over the question of how one could know for certain what another person was thinking, or sensing, or experiencing. With my girls snuggled around me, I wondered: could I know, by analogy to my own experience, what they were experiencing? Some of their sensory faculties were heightened, and some lessened, in comparison to mine.

Except in Juliet's case. Her sense of hearing was altogether absent: she heard nothing at all.

Though my life was still entwined with philosophy, I stopped teaching it. I was spending too much time with students each week rather than with my own family. I wanted to be home as Sophia and Juliet grew. And I wanted to continue to explore my family ancestry. I was no longer searching for relatives by database, or soaking up the flavors of shtetl life in books. My deaf ancestry was alive inside me, captured, conjured, by my imagination. I wasn't sure where it was taking me. But I had faith in it—a faith I hadn't had in any philosophical argument I'd ever constructed. I was groping my way back, my finger running along a last tattered string. To lengthen. Find strength in.

My far-flung relatives, blankened by distance in time and space, readily absorbed the dyes of my mind, and filled the white pages of my black, leather-bound journal. My imaginings pumped my writing as I pushed swings, peeled bananas, and read board books. As I spoke and I signed and I waited and I hoped for news that Juliet would be a candidate for the cochlear implant.

I answered a phone call one morning from an ear surgeon we had met at Boston Children's Hospital. She was calling to report that Juliet's MRI showed her cochlea to be structurally intact; this meant that implant surgery was an option for Juliet! Electrodes could be strung along the curvature of Juliet's inner ear, to do the work of her broken or bent or missing cilia. She could be made to "hear" through an electronic process; she could have access to language and sound.

The surgeon also had some results from Juliet's blood work. "Juliet's hearing loss is genetic," she said. "She has two deletions at the Connexin 26 gene site—35 del G and 167 del T." I scribbled it down. "Recessive gene mutations, one each from your husband and you. In all likelihood, Sophia has these too."

That afternoon, I went to my computer to look up Connexin 26. I found an online article about how, ordinarily, there are pairs at the gene site. Genetic mutations can cause deletions, with the result that there are singletons where pairs should be.

I gathered up the still-curling pages of my family chart, scattered across my desk amidst mugs of now cold tea. I stared at all the names, running this way and that, scribbled crosswise, scampering up and down family branches in desperate search of their other halves. The halves that make them whole. Make them hear. Make them heard.

Sophia and Juliet were heaped together in an over-stuffed beanbag chair in my study. Juliet was slipping off, clutching a fold of blue denim. I wedged myself in, yanked Juliet up from the side, and pulled both girls close around me.

◆ ◆ ◆

My most persistent childhood memory was of waiting: waiting for my mother while she "worked on herself" in front of her bathroom mirror. As if she might still bring her runaway father back? As if she might remake herself into someone worthy of his return? I'd never know all of the pieces, the shards she took up with a restorer's attention, to fashion herself whole.

Whenever I walked into the bathroom, my reflection bouncing into my mother's, she'd work on me, too. We could straighten my overly curly hair, she'd say. Her hairdresser could blow-dry it until it was fine and straight like baby grass. We could hunt down pleated shirts to narrow and conceal my growing breasts. Fix all that was wrong with me—my hair, my face, my body. My thoughts. My dreams.

Starving, I swallowed whatever she offered me. My mother was starving, too. Nothing could nourish her, fill her holes. As if literal food proved a mockery, she ate next to nothing. She reduced herself to a fragment, a figment. Less was more. But of course, less was less, as well.

Singletons where pairs should be.

My mother and I were the same, after all, in our wanting—she wanting him, me wanting her.

Her father did return after driving away. A year later, he appeared in the doorway of the Mount Vernon apartment. Hair tousled. Head cocked. All flair and fanfare. My mother couldn't hide her excitement, even as my grandmother's voice lilted with anger. He was beautiful, with almond eyes that brimmed with a like degree of hurt overlaying hope, overlaying hurt. A rally. They all rallied. But he couldn't stay.

My mother searched for her father years later, when I was in college—hired a private detective who tracked him down in Florida. She wrote him a long letter; she was in her fifties by then, a practicing therapist, a wife, and mother of four children. She wanted to see him, to introduce him to her husband, her children. He wrote back a one-sentence note: he was ill and he did not want her upsetting him. She was to keep away.

It was in my mother's crumbling reaction to her father's note that I realized what intricate structures she had been erecting so painstakingly in front of the mirror all those years. The foundations and powders to cover up and hide every perceptible flaw, in a room where she alone could not hear the feedback whistling from her damaged ears. Before this, I had perceived my mother's attempts to cover my blemishes as criticism of me, and her obsession to fix her own, as self-absorption. But I saw then that her intentions for both of us—we were one and the same in her heart—were fiercely protective. Before this, I had viewed my mother's withdrawals, her inattentions, as rejections of me. But I saw then that her retreat was just one more symptom of fatigue from her straining efforts to shore herself up, fill her holes, patch her half so that she might one day be made whole.

Sitting on the beanbag chair with Sophia and Juliet, I could see snowflakes drifting past the streetlights outside our window. A slight raise of my head, and I could see myself in the glass, my reflection. Fatigued. Fractured. I, too, knew the longing to be whole, for myself, for my family. The lure of powder to smooth the blemishes out. And I, too, knew the need to escape, to tune out my children. House chores, computer searches, journal writing sessions—they became justifications for retreat. I was drained and I yearned at times to be separate. But I also knew the need to hug tight, to clasp onto mother, even as she half-turned, inward. Away.

In the corner, high up on the bookshelf, I spotted a cluster of books by Martin Buber. I had read them in school. A baby gets its sense of self from its parent. I from Thou. A smile, a wide open "ah," a nose-kiss. Before individuation, the pure infectiousness of love; it bounces in the air between a mother and child's near-touching faces.

How could my mother help but falter? How could I help it?

Galicia, 1885

OUTSIDE THE HOUSE, A LIGHT snow dusts the ground. Elish and Herschel chase each other, dodging the frantic chickens. Inside, the youngest children play on the floor together, tangled like a heap of puppies. Pearl totters over rag dolls, a baby's shoe, tiny hands and feet. She surveys the mess, exhaustedly. Nellie is fourteen years old already, Bayla twelve. Like little mothers, they help feed, clean, and bounce the littler ones. When they go to the market now, Nellie and Bayla carry the small square chalkboard Rayzl gave them, and they carefully write out orders for meat and herbs. On the walk home, their hands move in Sign even when weighted down by baskets and children. All of the others hear, though Elish signs, too, and Herschel's stubby fingers have just begun to babble.

In the autumn, Nellie stands waiting for Herschel with a little cake from the bakery tucked in her basket. She peers through the window of his study class, the chilly air nipping at her ears. Herschel is the youngest in the room, just three years old. His hair is newly cropped, except for the earlocks.

Herschel is the family's bright hope for a scholar. So smart. Nellie watches how he talks, even recites daily blessings; how Pearl and Moshe beam with pride. Nellie can't help but flash with jealousy, knowing that she will never be adored, that she will never be a source of her parents' pride. She swallows her feelings like lumps, so that she can accept Herschel's eager embraces. Lately, he has become more and more attached to her—wanting her, watching her, following her everywhere and imitating her signs.

Early this morning, he tugged on her. He wanted only Nellie to walk him to school, no one else! Her parents couldn't stop fussing over him, puffing like peacocks as he left for his first day of school.

Back to collect him now, Nellie expects to see him still blushing with self-satisfaction. So why is he sitting quietly, withdrawn? Why is the teacher looking at him sternly, like he isn't answering his question?

Nellie can sense the din in the room, the heat; the opening and closing of books, the raising and lowering of hands— though not Herschel's. Nellie's eyes fix on his, and she follows their path: darting quickly from the other children's mouths to their eyes, mouths to eyes. She can see that his classmates are waiting for Herschel to speak; yet he remains silent.

As Nellie follows Herschel's eyes—his outsider, unknowing eyes—a knot deep down in her stomach rises to her chest, a cresting wave. Is it possible that her brother cannot hear the children around him, cannot hear his teacher? Can it be, that he has been delighting his parents at home by reciting what he'd previously learned, all the while losing his handle on sound?

Nellie stands outside the classroom, a certainty settling into her gut while thoughts spin in her head. She is unbearably cold, suddenly. The moment school lets out, Nellie grabs Herschel's hand tightly as he meanders down the steps toward her. The more she rushes him in their walk home, the more distractible he becomes, until she is nearly dragging him by one arm, his feet scraping the ground beneath them. She is walking so fast now that she practically slams into the front door.

Entering the house, Nellie is overcome by a surge of nausea, the air inside too hot, the lantern too bright after the brisk, darkening outside. She has rushed Herschel home as if to safety, but now home, she feels an urge to keep running.

Nellie settles her brother at the table with some cake, and goes to find Pearl in her room. Pearl looks confused; she can't follow Nellie's fast-moving hands. Nellie breathes in. Then she starts again. Just as Pearl did when they stood together over Bayla in her newborn bassinet, she points to her own ears, then to Herschel, who now stands in the doorway, and she shakes her head, "no."

Later that night, Nellie finds her mother rocking back and forth in her chair, her face laced with worry.

"Maybe Herschel can hide it, at least for now?" Nellie signs.

"What? How?" Pearl stops rocking.

"We can scrape the leather out from inside his shoe. He will feel the floor more with his feet. He'll know when someone is coming. If he remembers the words he has learned to speak . . . He can still speak . . ."

Pearl stares at her daughter's hands, tucked for the moment in her lap. For her boy—her Herschel—things will be more difficult.

"And I can show him how the floor shakes, Mama, how to figure out who is coming by how the floor shakes."

◆ ◆ ◆

When Pearl tells Moshe that Herschel is losing his hearing, Moshe just starts walking. Across the room and back again, across the room and back. Then he says words Pearl never thought she would hear.

"Pearl, I think we should leave Tasse."

"Leave Tasse?"

"Herschel will be a cast-aside here." Moshe waves his hand as if to push away a distant memory: his father's horse crisscrossing around a deaf man, dead in the road. "The rabbi told me the details of those discussions he had all those years ago. Do you remember?"

"Of course I remember. He said that Nellie would be accepted here. Look at what those peasant boys did to her and her sister."

"It will be far worse for Herschel. The boys in his class, they will taunt him, they will suppose he is stupid. It is one thing for the girls. But for Herschel—"

Pearl stares at her husband. Then she darts to her bedroom and begins rummaging through her trunk.

"Pearl, I don't mean we should start packing this moment!"

"I'm looking for a letter! That letter from Lill Baumann." Pearl retrieves the rumpled envelope from her trunk. The address reads: 1742 Union Street. Kings County New York. "Lill and Sam—they live in a big apartment building. Samuel found good work in a printing press. Maybe they can help us, just to get settled."

◆ ◆ ◆

They scrape together what they can. They scrimp and save, yet they haven't enough, not nearly enough, for all of them to go. How could Moshe have been so wrong in his figuring? Pearl stands at the wash basin, scrubbing a black pot. Her eyes burn. She lets the pot drop back into the basin, wipes her hands, and starts putting food out on plates.

Moshe is sounding out options. If only three can go, it should be Pearl and two children. Maybe Herschel and baby Sarah. The other children can stay put; the older ones can care for the littler ones, at least for a while. But no. Not Nellie or Bayla. They can't stay here without Pearl. Maybe Nellie and Bayla can go to Budapest, to the school for the Deaf, just until he can afford boat tickets.

Pearl puts a fist to her chest. Sends an imploring look Moshe's way. Moshe's eyes are cast downward. He is still considering. He can't pay for Rayzl's tutoring now, in any case.

Neighbors and friends tell cautionary tales, tales of people turned away at New York harbor, returned, barely alive, to a European port. The lame ones. The sick. Inspections officers and doctors check for difficulties. In 1885, even the land of opportunity has its limits. Pearl's mind circles, never to find a resting place.

Pearl is wary of the deaf school. Nellie and Bayla would be better off in America, with Herschel. Herschel's deafness will not be detectable to an inspector. Herschel knows how to read questions on lips, and he can speak out the answers. Nellie is at least cautious and watchful and she can control her voice. She can say her name; Rayzl has worked on this with her. Bayla is another story. Her vocalizations are loud and unintelligible. Bayla might be the tip-off that prevents their entry to America. Ach. It doesn't matter—the three deaf ones cannot manage such a trip by themselves. No.

Pearl and Moshe argue that night. And they argue each night until they are out of time. The morning that a carriage and three tickets are arranged, Moshe declares that Nellie, Herschel, and Elish will go together to America. Over Pearl's wails and objections, Bayla will travel with them as far as Budapest. She will be taken to the Jewish Children's Deaf Institute on Mexicoi Boulevard. The carriage will journey on to the train station, and from there they will travel to the port at Bremen. The others will stay behind until there is money enough to collect Bayla and travel to meet Nellie, Elish, and Herschel in America.

The house is complete chaos. Pearl stuffs extra scarves into an already bulging suitcase. Family and friends weep and kiss and hug the confused travelers. Moshe stalls the carriage driver, as people run in and out of the house. As Nellie, Bayla, Elish, and Herschel take their seats in the carriage, Pearl steps up after them. She takes their faces in her quivering hands, kisses their foreheads, her lips making promises of a quick reunion. When the horses start to whinny and stomp their feet, Pearl steps down. Nellie links her arms with Bayla, and Pearl wonders, suddenly, if perhaps the girls do not understand that they will be parting in Budapest, that Bayla will be left at the deaf school, and Nellie will take a train to the port at Bremen with Elish and Herschel. Pearl yells out to Elish, "Please explain, Elish—Nellie and Bayla will have to part, but they will be together soon. We will send for Bayla, and we will join you in America."

But as the carriage lurches forward, then turns sharply out of sight, Pearl is overtaken with anguish. Moshe comes to stand beside Pearl. He takes up her hand. Pearl yanks it away.

Inside the house, the four littlest children scuttle and run, they crawl and give chase; yet to Pearl, the house is vacant. Silent, amidst the din. How did they leave behind so much silence—they, who were largely silent themselves?

Moshe tries to placate her, he promises it will turn out all right. "How?" she asks. "How will it turn out all right?" Pearl stares at her husband. She has no faith left in him. He lives with his head in the clouds.

◆ ◆ ◆

Elish sits in the carriage, staring at her sisters. Nellie is bouncing Herschel on her lap, one arm twined around Bayla. Elish stalls. She gives herself a marker: I'll tell them when the carriage passes that tree. But the tree is well behind them now, and her eyes are scanning for a new marker. Finally, Elish takes a breath and taps her sisters on the knees to get their attention. As Nellie and Bayla comprehend her news, their heads shake violently. Tears drip dark spots onto their skirts. How could Mama have left it to her to tell them? Elish rages inside. As the carriage bumps along, Elish begins to cry; then Herschel, seeing the distraught faces of his three sisters, cries out too.

In Budapest, the carriage stops in front of a large brick building, its rows of arched windows with black wrought iron grates rising up four flights. Moshe had instructed the driver and paid him to escort Bayla into the office of the Headmaster. He nearly has to pry Bayla out of Nellie's grip and drag her, rumpled and shaking, into the school. The three in the carriage are still crying, as he hoists himself back up and takes hold of the reins.

◆ ◆ ◆

In a dank corner, below deck on the ship, Nellie sits huddled with Elish and Herschel. Day and night. Day and night. They hardly have room to stretch out their legs. All around them, passengers are gripped with seasickness. For Nellie, it is not the turbulent motions of the ship that nauseate her, but the foul smells all around—the body odors, the vomit, the urine clinging to the sides of open buckets. Nellie offers Elish and Herschel food from the satchel that Pearl carefully packed for them. She herself can scarcely eat. She winds a shawl—Bayla's shawl—around her nose and mouth, and breathes in her missing sister.

Nellie takes knitting in hand, but her stitches bunch and pull. She rips them out, stows the yarn in her bag. Her temples pound with grief, as Elish tutors her to speak out answers to questions she may be asked by an Inspections Officer.

Weeks pass, and finally the boat docks in New York harbor. Filthy and ragged, they weave their way out of the ship's steerage compartment, unsteadily up the stairs to the outer decks, and finally, by barge, onto a pier in New York Bay. In a long winding line, they step into Castle Gardens. Uniformed doctors are everywhere, inspecting the passengers' scalps for lice, their nails for fungus. Nellie yelps at the sight of a doctor brandishing a gleaming buttonhook, a man's face twisting in pain as his eyelid is turned up. She clutches tight to Elish and Herschel.

As they approach the front of their line, numbers pinned to their coats, an inspection officer barks a soundless question at Nellie. Her name, she thinks. He must have asked her to state her name. She practiced this day and night on the ship. Now she shapes her lips, her tongue flat against the bridge of her mouth for the "n", then poking out a bit for the "l." She manages the four syllables "Nel-lie Wert-heim," her belly pressing down on her bowel as her breath recedes. Her sounds—were they all *right, she wonders? Because the man's eyes have widened and his eyebrows are up.*

Quickly, Elish steps forward, saying in Yiddish that she, her sister, and brother, have traveled together to meet Samuel Baumann. If Samuel Baumann isn't waiting for them, they are to make their way to 1742 Union Street in Brooklyn. She picks up Herschel, as if to be on her way to Union Street that very moment. The inspector looks at the threesome uncertainly, a piece of chalk balancing between two dusty white fingers. Herschel blinks and smiles, his eyes puffy, his skin reddened from the sea air. The inspector asks to see Herschel walk. Elish sets Herschel down, steps several lengths back, then beckons him to come. As Herschel walks to Elish, the officer turns back to Nellie, hesitating. Then, with a brush of his arm, he waves them along into the interior rotunda. They gather their belongings, and Elish tells a registering clerk their names, their old residence, and their destination.

Nellie, Elish, and Herschel squeeze onto a wooden bench next to three elderly women cloaked in scarves. Their eyes search the faces of each passerby as their feet dangle in America's hope-suspended air. When Nellie raises her hands to sign something to Herschel, Elish presses them against Nellie's lap, a pleading look on her face. As it is, a clerk has looked over at them more than once. Four hours pass. Then five. Herschel has fallen asleep, his head cocked against Nellie's shoulder. A large man with a bushy grey beard and a wide black hat approaches the bench. In Yiddish, he asks Elish her name. When she tells him, he smiles in relief and points a finger to his chest. "I am Samuel Baumann. My wife, Lill, is an old friend of your mother's. You children gather your things. You're to stay with us!"

Massachusetts, March 2004

SOPHIA AND JULIET HAD SEPARATE bedrooms but I put them together at night. They would settle cozily in Juliet's bright purple room, decorated with Sophia's white painted hand prints and lit gently with a lamb night-light.

When they fell asleep, I'd trudge upstairs to my bedroom and undress before the mirror. Though months had passed since my surgery, I wasn't at peace with the thick pink scar that lay across the soft white skin of my breast. A deep vacancy still inside, coarsely sewn over, giving the impression of being healed, of being filled—yet gaping.

Bill and I were like factory workers on different shifts, managing the endless conveyor belt of needs. Feedings. Diaper changes. Story readings. Strolls around the block. Juliet was still waking through the night. Sophia was testy and oppositional during the day. Lucca was getting sicker. Both girls were low weight, and I had morphed myself into a combination short order cook and pastry chef. Amidst it all, we had big decisions still to make for Juliet, and for us. I felt drained, empty.

◆ ◆ ◆

Bill started playing with Juliet in the early morning, so I could get more sleep. When Juliet cried out, Bill would take her into the playroom to look at books, to play with puzzles, and to dance. Bill twirled Juliet and tickled her. He bundled her up and trudged with her out in the snow. They were the first customers for hot bagels at the bagel shop. He walked her to the river, to the boathouse, to the marshes where the heron came. He jogged her to the farmer's market, then plopped her at my bedside with a big bouquet of flowers. Bill became Juliet's "adventure" man; when he entered a room, she looked around for her shoes and coat, and for clues as to where they might be going.

Bill was my "adventure" man, too; I looked at him and wondered where in the roller-coaster ride we were at this or that precise moment. Over time, and with a little more sleep, the twists felt smoother; the heaves less sudden. We hired a babysitter so we could take quiet walks together. We mulled around used bookstores, found our way back to the Indian restaurant we liked on our first visit to Northampton. We inched our way back in, closer.

♦ ♦ ♦

The Boston ear surgeon gave us the names of the three companies that manufactured cochlear implants: Cochlear, MED-EL, and Advanced Bionics. Late one night, I looked up the Cochlear company on the Internet. Link by link, I found my way to their implant simulation site. Alan Alda was narrating. I was instantly calmed by his familiar voice, and though his hair was grey and he wore a dark suit, he had the relaxed, youthful manner of the army doctor he played all those years on *M*A*S*H**. After a few minutes, Alda's crisp visual image broke up into a fragmented blur of tiny rectangles, with parts fading out of focus, others darkening. I could just barely recognize Alda's face when the screen froze and I heard Alda's voice proudly announce that *this*—this disjointed mess—was the visual analogue of the cochlear implant.

Next, a lady's voice piped in to give the auditory simulation. "I like to play tennis," she said, and I heard it first the "regular" way. Then I heard it simulated, as it sounded to someone with a cochlear implant. The perky, even melodious phrase "I like to play tennis" was mutilated, grotesquely transformed. *Had Darth Vader joined Demi Moore and the Wicked Witch of the West to create this raspy, witchy, all-throat sound?* I sat stiffly in front of the computer screen.

Then I woke Bill. Were we going to drill into Juliet's tiny skull for *this*? Could we never expect Juliet to hear the timbre of our voices, or to distinguish between voices, or experience the beauty of music?

For the next several days, Bill and I went to the Clarke School playground at recess and we watched and listened to the children with cochlear implants. There was not a single Darth-Demi-Gulch sound-alike in the bunch. The implanted children heard language and spoke clearly. On the sideline of a soccer game, I chatted with the Clarke teachers about the implant technology. It was not without challenges—it would be hard to hear in noisy places and localizing sound would be difficult—but the implant, if successful, could bring a profoundly deaf child access to spoken language and other sound.

Once again, we faced a decision between manual and oral communication approaches, between Deafness and Hearing, as we had with Sophia three years ago. But whereas Sophia's hearing loss was "severe," Juliet's was "profound." To be "oral," Juliet would have to undergo the cochlear implant surgery, and then, with extensive training, her "hearing" would proceed electronically. Still, there were many considerations that we faced in Sophia's case that were the same in Juliet's: only .02 percent of people in the US are fluent in American Sign Language, compared to the 99.98 percent of people who use spoken language. If we could place Juliet in the hearing world, we would be giving her the chance to communicate with the larger, hearing population. And not only with the larger population, but with *Sophia*, who was acquiring some Sign, but it was clear that she learned—and flourished—as a hearing, speaking, "oral" child. And with *us*: we wanted our relationship, our intimacy, with Juliet.

There were arguments against cochlear implants, but to me their force was more applicable to the "deaf of deaf"—deaf children born of deaf parents. The thought that deaf children "belonged in" and would flourish more in the Deaf community made a great deal of sense to me if the child's extended family was deaf and part of that community. It made less sense if a child's parents and family were outside the Deaf community. I understood that in the past, deaf children often found solace from isolation by leaving behind their hearing families and joining a separate, Deaf community. But I felt it was imperative for *our* family to find a way to share in the same community, one way or another. We also came across the "autonomy" argument—that parents should not impose a decision on a child, but rather should wait until the child can make it. But oral language development required early stimulation of the neural pathways to the brain. To wait for years for a child's autonomous decision to get an implant would be to drastically minimize its chances of success. And the argument that cochlear implants might relegate a child to a "no man's land"—if the implant was not entirely successful or if the child's speech was less than fully intelligible, he might find himself in neither the hearing world nor the Deaf world—didn't bear out in the current statistics of young and otherwise healthy implant recipients.

One day, in the hall of the Clarke School, I met a mother of two implanted deaf boys. I was surprised to hear her say: "When my younger son failed the hearing test, I just prayed that he was deaf enough for the cochlear implant." She went on to talk about the difficulty of being too deaf for effectual hearing aids but not deaf enough for implants. She enumerated the troubles her boys had encountered with hearing aids—amplified background noise and feedback, troubles we knew all too well from Sophia—and she extolled the implants as having fewer "interferences" than hearing aids. The mother was thrilled by her sons' successes. As I stood there talking, with Juliet perched in my arms, I could see that Juliet's eyes were tracking the movements of our lips, working to decipher our conversation. Juliet could be restrung! Correcting for the broken, bent, or missing cilia in her ear, a run of wire could be wound along the curls of her cochlea, with twenty-four channels working to transmit auditory information to her brain. She could hear language. And she could speak. *Something Pearl couldn't have dreamed of for her girls.*

We decided to proceed with the surgery, and we scheduled it for the day Juliet became eligible for it: the day she would turn one year old.

◆ ◆ ◆

Our Deaf teacher, Cynthia, continued to come to our house every Saturday morning. Before she arrived, Sophia, Juliet, and I made small but special preparations for her visit: homemade cookies, or fruit salad, or hand-drawn cards.

One Saturday, after a Sign lesson, I told Cynthia that we had scheduled Juliet for cochlear implant surgery. I told her that we wanted to continue to Sign, too. Cynthia froze her face. Actually, she froze half of it. Somehow, she immobilized the left half of her face, while the right half took on distorted, changing forms of expression. Her right eyebrow arched, her right cheek dimpled, her right lip curled down, all while the left half of her face remained expressionless and flat. I knew she was illustrating the paralysis that the implant surgery could cause. The surgery is done in the vicinity of a facial nerve, and the surgeon had cited facial paralysis as a rare but possible side effect. I felt my own face freeze in response to Cynthia's illustration, and we said a rushed good-bye.

After that, Cynthia stopped coming. She didn't answer our emails, our faxes, or our TTY calls. Almost weekly, Sophia would ask, "Where's Cynthia? What happened to Cynthia?"

We didn't explain to Sophia that our decision to give Juliet surgical access to sound was an offense to Cynthia. An insult in its suggestion that deafness was something to fix—eradicate, even—no matter its risks. Selfish of us, according to Cynthia, presumptuous to "change" our baby, to embark on a surgery, when she was healthy and well. We told Sophia that Cynthia had a scheduling conflict. Sophia was three years old, and we wanted to buffer her for as long as possible from the fractures and judgments that everywhere marked the Hearing/Deaf divide.

Cynthia's reaction was, I could only imagine, rooted in the deep pain caused by a long history of wrongful treatment marked by discrimination, marginalization, and invalidation. What beauty in language, and what sophistication in culture the Deaf had wrought from this pain, what pride they could claim, was now threatened, even from the inside. Despite the gain of new rights, the Deaf community was losing membership. With cochlear implants, deaf people were learning to listen and speak. Children like ours were gaining a world—a hearing world—as the world of the signing Deaf, with its rich and vibrant culture, was shrinking.

I tried for months to reach Cynthia, but I never heard from her again.

In time, we found another teacher, someone who lived Deaf, without hearing or speaking but who, without question, honored our decision to do what we considered best for our children. Her name was Kathie. Her eyes and hair were the matching color of nutmeg, and she wore country dresses with small print flowers and colored bows. She had two sons of her own, both deaf, and she radiated motherly nurturance. Sophia and Juliet warmed to her instantly.

Often, when Kathie arrived, she'd pick up one of the girls' favorite books—*Goldilocks and the Three Bears* or *Lily's Big Day* or *Bread and Jam for Frances*—and sign it out for Sophia and Juliet with grand expression and drama. The girls sat snuggled in her lap, mesmerized.

Kathie walked through the playroom, showing us the sign-names for the girls' puzzles and board games and stuffed animals. In the kitchen, she taught us the signs for their favorite foods: nectarines, sugar cookies, spaghetti, ice cream. In the bathroom: their bath toys, their toothbrushes, their "silly strawberry" toothpaste. Sophia and Juliet acquired a small, practical vocabulary. Bill learned enough to communicate with the girls at bath and bed time. I continued on, vowing to keep Sign an option for the girls as they grew older, hoping they would have the chance to forge ties and friendships within the Deaf community over their lifetimes.

In my list of notes for Juliet's surgeon—we were on a countdown now, with Juliet's surgery just six weeks away— I added a question about how, precisely, Juliet's facial nerves would be monitored throughout the operation.

Massachusetts, August 2004

A WEEK BEFORE JULIET'S SURGERY, we went to Vermont. Best to keep our minds off the impending operation. We'd kayak, eat the local bread pudding, swim in a lake, and ride horses. I'd read in a lounge chair while the girls glopped up the deck with the rubbery but allegedly non-toxic blue, pink, yellow, and green nail polish they'd gotten in a birthday party goody bag. I was excited to dig into my new copy of the *Best American Essays*.

As the smell of last night's burnt marshmallows wafted by, and the lake gently lapped atop the rocks below, I opened up the crisp volume to the table of contents. Atul Gawande's name caught my attention. Wasn't he a doctor? I had heard him speak on NPR once. Before I could stop myself, I was engrossed in Gawande's essay: "The Learning Curve," all about how medical residents learn by practicing on patients, inevitably making mistakes along the way. Gawande described his own learning curve, a series of failures on his way to successes, while illuminating ethical tensions between providing patients with the best possible care and training doctors for the future. As I read, I slumped down in the deck chair and my left shoulder blade became painfully lodged between two narrow wood slats. I glanced over at Juliet, her tiny fingers and toes entirely covered in a sticky rainbow of glop. What was the point in even trying to relax?

I reached for my cell phone and checked for service. One tiny bar appeared. I dialed anyway, punching in the now-familiar number of the cochlear implant coordinator at Childrens' Hospital. I asked to know who the surgical residents were, the ones who would be assisting our carefully chosen, experienced surgeon.

"They don't actually assign the residents until the night before," she said.

"What?"

"Even the surgeon won't know until the morning of the surgery."

I was silent.

"Look, it will probably be one of three. I can give you their names if it will make you feel better."

"Yes, I want their names." In my head I was already planning out a trip to the computer center in town, where I would Google them.

The coordinator patiently spelled them out for me. "They are *all* excellent. They don't get placed here if they aren't. Besides, the doctor watches them very carefully."

"Watches them make their mistakes?" I couldn't help blurting out. "I'm sorry. But I'd feel much better if I knew exactly what part of the surgery the surgeon performs and what part the residents perform. And how many times the residents have performed their parts, and how success-fully."

"You can call the surgeon if you like."

"And what about the anesthesiologist? Do you know who the anesthesiologist will be? And has that person been informed that Juliet weighs less than most cats?"

I turned to see Bill's wide, apprehensive eyes staring at me. Like I had finally lost my mind.

◆ ◆ ◆

In Vermont, Lucca's pee became a thick stream of blood, her face, a knot of anxiety. She whimpered and cried and walked in frantic circles in anticipation of sitting down. Her quality of life was diminishing before our eyes. The day we got home, we arranged for a babysitter to take the girls out of the house, and called for the vet to come. While we waited, Bill and I sat together on the living room floor, petting Lucca and kissing her. She was our softest-coated, brown eyed girl who centered us, who took us out into the air—morning, noon, and night—basking in sun, bounding in snow, wincing in rain. Before she got sick, she sat patiently, equidistantly, between us as we read or worked in the house. And she slept beside us, her paws bouncing, as she dreamed her dog-dreams in our midst. The night she got sprayed by a skunk, years before we had kids, Bill and I slept in sleeping bags with her in the garage. She kept us up into the wee hours, her tail thumping against our blue nylon bags, wagging out her excitement at this novel bedtime arrangement.

We hugged Lucca as the vet put the needle into her leg, but she jerked her leg away, and jerked it away again and again. Until the vet stood up and said that he would bring tranquilizer drugs for us to give her overnight and return tomorrow.

How to get through this stolen day, this night, but tend to Lucca, to Sophia, and to Juliet—all in constant neediness? The next morning, Bill urged me to leave the house with the girls before the vet's second arrival. Lucca was already tranquilized, but upon seeing me walk toward the stair, she lifted herself up to follow, then fell down, legs splayed. I gave Lucca final kisses and I left swallowing my tears, with Sophia and Juliet in tow. Driving in the car, a moment came when the cloudless blue sky broke open in my mind, and I knew that Lucca was gone. She left without my hand on her thick furry side, without my breath in her ear. The loss, all my own.

Massachusetts, September 2004

IN THE CHILL OF EARLY MORNING, Juliet's first birthday, Bill and I settled Sophia, still in her pajamas, into my parents' hotel room down the hall from ours. Then we bundled Juliet in her fleece coat and crossed the busy Boston street to Children's Hospital. I clutched Juliet tightly as we walked, shielding her from the wind as I could not shield her from the risks of the operation she was about to undergo. In the pre-op room at 6 a.m., she was one of at least fifteen babies facing surgery.

Awake most of the previous night, watching Juliet sleep, all I could think was: *she is intact.* The sounds reverberating in my ears—the rumble of the ice machine, the shuffling of feet down the hall, the hum of the heater—why were they so important? Juliet understood the world as well as any one year old, and she was happy, bonded to us, related. How crazy were we to have a surgeon invade her head, drill into her tiny skull, weave an electrode array around the curls of her cochlea—all to bring her into the hearing world?

Diminished by my uncertainties, it was all I could do to follow the directions of the nurses. I put on scrubs so that I could carry Juliet into the operating room and hold her as they administered the anesthesia. As I put the blue mask over my mouth in preparation, Juliet, her playful eyes sparkling, yanked the mask off in a peek-a-boo game.

In the operating room, I held Juliet tight, warm against me, as the doctors briskly shoved a black rubber mask against her face. Her muffled gasps were swallowed up, her fight dissolving as she went limp in my arms. Quickly, the doctors took her and ushered me out of the room. Bill was waiting for me as I weaved my way, flushed and dazed, to the end of the hallway.

The surgery could take up to five hours. As we searched for an empty cluster of chairs in the waiting area, we recognized a mother and daughter from a pre-op appointment two weeks earlier. I looked on as Bill engaged the daughter, played Pacman with her. I filled with admiration for Bill, for his kindness toward this worried little girl—her twin brother was in surgery—but it only punctuated my loneliness.

I called Sophia on my cell phone. She was watching cartoons. I told her I'd call again when Juliet was out of surgery.

"She'll have a big bandage on her head?"

"Yes, like in the pictures I showed you."

"Because they're making a cut in her head?"

"Yes."

"Will it hurt?"

From Sophia's tone, I half suspected that she hoped it would.

"I need to go now, Sophia. Have fun with Grandma and Grandpa. I love you."

I hunkered into a seat, and I started to open a skein of wool. I was going to use my hands, crochet a scarf, allow the rhythm of my movements to calm my bursting head. Somehow, though, my opening of the skein yielded an immense tangle of wool. I looked at Bill, now sitting beside me, reading the newspaper. I asked him if he would help me unravel the mess of knots and he said "No," he couldn't bear to, it would unravel *him*. Next to him, but alone, I sat for the next several hours, trying to untangle the wool, my eyes burning.

The attending nurse cheerily updated us with: "they're still drilling" (into Juliet's skull, that is) at the forty-five minute mark, at the one and a half hour mark, and unbelievably, at the two hour and fifteen minute mark. I couldn't help overhearing conversations about cancerous tumors and heart defects. Another mother, sitting a few seats away, burst into tears.

Sometime during the fourth hour, I looked down and noticed that my wedding ring was not on my finger; it must have slipped off. I searched the waiting room, then I searched the bathroom, the cafeteria, everywhere I had been that morning. How could it be lost? I rummaged through my bag, then dumped the entire contents onto the chair next to me. My ring was nowhere among the papers about implants, the sticky notes with friends' cell phone numbers, my wallet, random coins, paper clips, and the sparkles fallen from Sophia's barrettes. With quaking fingers, I squeezed my hand into the narrow inside zipper pocket. There, my fingers twisted tight around the cool braided gold. I put the ring on, reassembled my bag, stowed the skein of wool, and pressed my back into the chair for the remainder of the wait.

From down the hall, I saw the surgeon loping toward us. His blue scrub mask was pushed back on his forehead, and he was grinning a toothy smile. Bill and I had liked him since our first consultation. He told us that his own son had needed ear surgery as an infant—a surgery that he'd had to sit out. Now he came to lean against the arm of a nearby chair, his legs stretched out in front of him.

"The surgery was extremely successful. We were able to thread the electrode array very high up along the curvature of Juliet's cochlea. She is going to have access to all channels. We tested the implant mechanism and it's working. When the surgery wound heals, in about a month, the audiologist will program her external processor. I'd like to see Juliet in about three weeks."

I was elated, and suddenly embarrassed that in the same time it took the surgeon to give Juliet a cochlear implant, all I accomplished was unraveling a skein of wool.

In the recovery room, Juliet's head was bandaged thickly, her face swollen, her eyebrows pressed low. Asleep, she looked agitated, like a boxer in a fight. She awoke in a fury, screaming and punching, a detoxifying maniac as the anesthesia worked its way out of her body. I gathered her up but the weight of her bandage threw us both off-balance. She nearly flipped out of my arms, she was so top-heavy. I jostled her into a cradle position, careful not to stretch the many tubes and wires connecting her to monitors. Juliet raged inconsolably, then suddenly, abruptly, fell asleep.

Twenty minutes later she awoke again in a fit, her arms and legs flailing, then she tumbled back to sleep. I held her through the night, through countless ragings and sleeps, cramped in the hospital crib-cage meant only for her. In the early dawn, I perceived the smooshed and crooked beginnings of a smile. Juliet stood herself up, lifted her blanket to cover her face, and resumed our earlier game of peek-a-boo.

◆ ◆ ◆

A month after the surgery, we drove back to the hospital so that the audiologist could "turn on" Juliet's sound. An external processor would be programmed by computer, first very softly, then later with gradual increases in volume. Like a dimmer switch on lights, it was important to be gradual with Juliet, so that she would *like* sound, since she could take her processor off (and stop hearing) if she didn't. Before we got into the car to go, the phone rang. It was Jan, from Clarke.

"Are you ready?"

"I don't know," I said.

"You should be prepared for Juliet to cry. Lots of babies cry."

"I know."

"Or she might become agitated."

"OK."

"I just want you to know, Juliet is not going to respond today the way you want her to. What you want is for her to hear her first sound, turn to you, and say: thank you so much!"

In fact, Juliet's reaction to sound was far more wondrous. In the cochlear implant mapping room, its door marked with a child's geometric drawing of a cochlea, Bill and I wrapped our arms around Juliet as the audiologist programmed the external processor on the computer. The external processor consisted of an earpiece, shaped like a behind-the-ear hearing aid, with one wire attaching to a magnetic disk the size of a quarter and another wire attaching to a small box with a control panel. Juliet's earpiece was blue, like Sophia's hearing aids, and now the audiologist attached a snazzy pink stripe to its top. The magnetic disc was brown, and it glommed onto Juliet's head like a magnet onto a refrigerator: *glup*.

The audiologist instructed us to be completely silent. She turned the system "on," then handed Juliet a drum and a stick. Juliet whacked the drum, then jumped back like a startled animal at the sound of the boom. She searched our faces with wide questioning eyes. She beat the drum again. Boom! Then, with a wild thrust of her head, Juliet laughed.

Juliet used the drum stick to beat other things: the audiologist's pant leg made almost no sound, the metal file cabinet made a loud clanging boom, the wood chair back sounded different from the thick wood table top. Juliet, at thirteen months, was a scientist, studying and experimenting with sound.

According to the audiologist, all sounds would come in as beeps and blips at first. It would take months before the neural pathways between Juliet's auditory nerve and her brain would be forged and able to translate the input into meaningful sound. Months before "moo" could be distinguished from "quack" and pinned on its rightful farm speaker. And months before Juliet would turn at the calling of her name. But Juliet's excitement carried us through. At home, she was thrilled to hear the sizzle of an egg in the frying pan, the rush of water through the faucet. She prompted us to sing songs, to "moo" and to "quack," to turn on music, to attend to the many noises we ordinarily delegated to the background and ignored.

We poured milk into Rice Krispies cereal, and we bent our heads low to the bowl. *Snap! Crackle! Pop!* We jingled bicycle bells: *Jing, Jing!* Rang doorbells: *Ding Dong!* Honked horns: *Beep Beep!* We placed and received calls on our toy phone: *Rrrring Rrrring Rrrring!* We bought and sold stuffed animals with our toy cash register: *Ring; Bonk* (the money drawer sliding open). We played "Jungle"—*Roar!*—and "Farm"—*Cockadoodledoo!* We sounded off harmonicas, drums, recorders, a kazoo. A whoopy cushion.

Juliet reawakened us all again to the wonder of hearing. Her joy chased away our worries that our decision was self-ish or presumptuous. Even if it was these things, it was not *wrong*. Juliet reveled in sound.

◆ ◆ ◆

We hunkered into our work. And we hunkered into our wait. Who knew what Juliet was processing? Or what she might sound like when she had heard enough to venture into speech? I thought often of that computer simulation I'd heard: that croaky sentence, "I like to play tennis." Was Juliet's hearing really like that? For a week, when I had laryngitis, I was especially curious. Perhaps through an implant, my raspy voice was inverted, so I finally sounded like my usual self?

Each morning, we put on Juliet's implant proces-sor. I also stuck a high-volume hearing aid into her non-implanted ear. Set at highest volume, the hearing aid might give her access to some sounds—most likely low frequency sounds and sound patterns. If it worked at all, she'd hear these through the normal hearing process, rather than the implant's electronic one. Juliet objected to the aid, but I persisted in putting it in. Through her fits, I rasped in my best Demi-Darth-Gulch voice. Any chance to round out Juliet's auditory experience was worth it.

Bill made us breakfast—the girls liked his "crispy" scrambled eggs—and then went upstairs to work. He was telecommuting now, working in our attic for a national child advocacy organization based in Seattle. Sophia put on her own hearing aids, and got ready for preschool. Then, I whisked Sophia and Juliet down the block in our double stroller to Sophia's school. Once Sophia was settled into her classroom—having shown us her paper weavings, her popsicle stick fairies, her plastic cup of grass on the windowsill—Juliet and I ambled our way home, missing Sophia already. Back inside, to keep things cheery, I chased Juliet around our house. "I'm going to get you, Juliet," I yelled. And with exaggerated, booming steps, I ran after her, as she scuttled ahead of me, squealing.

We had the perfect house for a chase: an 1800s New England house built around a central staircase. One day in snowy February, we ran round and round, through the dining room, the kitchen, the family room, the living room, then back into the entry—the "foyer" as the realtor had called it. Every time I raced into the kitchen, my toes knocked into the slightly raised threshold, bruising even through my chunky blue socks, while Juliet galloped over the rise each time with the precision of a cat.

At one point the tea kettle whistled and I broke the chase for a quick hearing lesson. I stood still in the kitchen until Juliet knocked into me, catapulted from her whole lap lead, and as she caught her breath I pointed out the high-pitched whistle, blowing on and on, thick steam shooting up at the kitchen cabinets. "I hear it," I said, pointing to my ears. Then I switched off the stove, moved the kettle to a cool burner and resumed the chase, offering Juliet the lead, trailing in the sea of squeal and laughter that floated in from the room ahead.

The run became a blur of changing colors—blue in the living room, gold in the kitchen—and a dance of white as we passed the wavy window glass. Time-out had to be called several more times because Juliet's processor magnet slipped off a lot, dragged down by the weight of her processor, flapping in a pocket I'd hastily sewn onto her t-shirt.

Juliet took the Time-outs like a puppy halted mid-nip to scratch an itch. Her eyes sparkled each time the chase resumed, her reddish hair wispy and loose, slipping out of her top-knot. At one point, as I gained on her, sock skating down the burgundy stretch of dining room, I called out "I'm going to get you, Juliet!" and she turned her head to look at me.

I stopped in my tracks like Roadrunner.

"Juliet?" I ventured again. By now Juliet was smiling a huge smile—she had heard and recognized her name.

"Juliet!" I choked and I scooped her into my arms. "I got you, Juliet. I got you. I've gotten you."

Juliet nuzzled me with her flushed cheek. Then she squirmed out of my embrace, and resumed running.

Massachusetts, February 2005

TO SUPPORT US IN OUR WORK with Juliet, we had a team of clinicians, many of whom had worked with Sophia, all by now our dear friends, our de facto therapists, our lifelines, our heroes.

Marilyn, Juliet's audiologist, checked and updated Juliet's implant mapping programs to ensure that she was hearing. Jan worked with Juliet on listening—attending to sound, discriminating, imitating, turn-taking. Jean worked with Juliet on all manner of communicating—vocalizing, signaling, and gesturing. Kathie worked with all of us on Signing.

Just as we'd done with Sophia, we focused our speech work with Juliet on single power words: *UP, DOWN, OPEN, CLOSE.* We talked incessantly. *"Do you want to come UP? I'll pick you UP. Now you're UP! UP, UP, UP . . ."* When Juliet had enough, we settled her into the center of a big blue blanket, took up the corners and swung her back and forth, back and forth. She squealed with added delight when Sophia climbed in too, and we swayed them together in a heavy heap, steady and low. Their laughter drowned out our expertly articulated counting, our overly-annunciated "*wheeees.*"

No matter how eagerly we awaited Juliet's first spoken word, it would (evidently) come in its own time, regardless of our prompting and prodding.

At nighttime, when I wrote in my journal, I could see my uncertainty steering the way. We'd crossed worlds for Juliet, yet with no sense of what lay ahead. No sense of what she was hearing, or when she might speak, or how she experienced this new world of sound that we turned on and off with the flick of a magnet. In the universe of my ancestors, of Nellie and Bayla, I had no more certainty about what they experienced. Only my hopes and my fears. My need to forge on.

New York, 1885

NELLIE CLASPS HERSCHEL'S HAND *and yanks him out of the way of the morning stampede as men in black hats and coats, white fringes billowing at their sides, rush through the streets to work. When the foot traffic slows, Nellie and Herschel resume their walk, dawdling down Union Street. Herschel is calmer when they are outside. Inside Lill's apartment, he rages: "Mama, Mama, Mama." He fusses and cries; he even kicks the little wood blocks that Samuel gave him. Nellie can't seem to calm him.*

Now just a few feet from Lill's building, Nellie thinks: perhaps one more time, they can walk around the block. But no more buying! They already spent on a little cake at the bakery and a bag of roasted chickpeas from a pushcart peddler. She'd have to steer him away from the steaming sweet potatoes, the open cracker barrels. Just fresh air this time around.

At the street corner, a mail carriage passes by. Nellie wonders how long it will take for a letter to arrive, how long before she will get word that Bayla and the others are journeying to America. Nellie imagines Bayla in a cramped dormitory room with unknown schoolmates and strict schoolmasters. No one like Rayzl, with a writing tablet tucked under her arm.

Instead of looping back to the apartment now, Nellie lifts Herschel and carries him on her hip, past the butcher, past the tailor, and even past the bookbinder. Elish told her of a factory several blocks to the east with lots of girls, sewing. If she can get work there, and do a fine job, perhaps Bayla will be welcome, too, when she arrives. Nellie rushes along, her eyes fixed on the tiny metal shards embedded in the sidewalk. At the edge of a small park, in the center of the next city block, Nellie looks up, then stops abruptly. Herschel nearly falls from her hip.

Up on a park bench, a girl stands at her mother's shoulder height. Her hands soar in fast, intentional flight. Nellie can see that the girl's movements are not just gestures accompanying speech, but signs, a language. Nellie stands unmoving. She watches for several minutes, trying to decipher the dialect of the girl's hands. But now the girl stops. It is the mother's turn and she seems to be chastising her daughter: the girl mustn't throw the crumbs they brought for the pigeons upon storefront steps, nor should she throw them at dogs being walked in the park. The mother's young face is kind but stern as she sets out the breadcrumb rules, and the girl signals that she understands. Growing restless, the girl turns away, pivoting nearly in a full circle, when her eyes brush past Nellie and lock onto Herschel.

Nellie takes a breath and sets Herschel down. The girl jumps down from the bench and faces him. Together, but almost as if they are carrying bundles between their legs, the children inch closer until they are just a few feet away. The mother turns to them now, and as the two children stare widely at each other, Nellie signs to the woman. The woman signs back—her name is Sylvia, and she is pleased, very pleased, to meet Nellie!

When they part, Sylvia invites Nellie to meet them again later in the week. With Herschel re-hoisted up on her hip, Nellie reels. She feels larger in her body than she has in months. She tightens her clasp around her little brother, inhaling the sweet oil of his hair, the soft floury smell of his cheek.

Approaching the factory door, Nellie sets Herschel down and motions for him to wait outside. A saggy man with tired grey eyes and unkempt grey hair looks Nellie up and down as she walks in. Nellie pantomimes sewing. She points to the tiny, delicate stitches on her shirt, then at her own hands and again gestures a stitch. The manager begins talking, but Nellie cannot follow what he is saying. She scans the room helplessly. Girls look up from their tables, then glue their eyes back to their work. The man is used to immigrants. He takes Nellie's arm, squeezing a little too tight, and walks her to a sewing table with an empty chair. He hands her a scrap of lacy cotton and a threaded needle. Nellie carefully stitches a seam in close, even stitches. The man nods and motions for her to remain seated. Nellie settles into the seat, then abruptly she stands, suddenly remembering that Herschel is waiting outside for her. She must go. Boldly, Nellie shakes her head apologetically and rushes out the door. The man watches from the doorway as Nellie sweeps Herschel into her arms and runs down the block. In heaving breaths, she returns twenty minutes later, and claims her seat. The manager frowns, but places a large wire frame and a bolt of white cotton fabric on her table. Nellie will learn to sew corsets.

◆ ◆ ◆

Late at night, Nellie practices writing Yiddish words in a loopy hand. She longs to tell Bayla all about her new job and about Sylvia—how they meet at the park most evenings; how Herschel chases little Sarah around the fountain. They throw crumbs at the silvery blue pigeons that approach haltingly, never blinking their sharp, pea green eyes. In those dusky hours, with fountain water misting Herschel's black curls and flushed cheeks, the glaze lifts from his eyes, and his heart isn't so heavy with longing for Mama and Papa. And Nellie is hopeful then that things will be all right, that she can manage until they arrive.

Nellie sets aside her practice sheet and places a piece of fine writing paper on the wobbly table near her bedside. Her hand shakes as she begins her letter.

> dear Bayla,
> I wait wait you.
> Here buildings to sky! People everywhere, moving fast.
> Lill and Samuel let us stay, their home our home also.
> Job I got. what? sewing. I one of many girls, all of us sewing.
> Met woman, deaf also. Name Sylvia.
> Last I saw you, crying. Horse-driver-man took you from carriage.
> I wrote to Mama letter, need Mama, Papa, family join us here.
> Need Bayla with me here.
> Biggest hugs,
> Nellie

Nellie inspects her crooked, ugly penmanship. She knows that the language of her hands doesn't match up with written language. If only she'd had more time with Rayzl, to learn. She carefully folds the letter into an envelope—for Bayla it is all right—and in the morning, she presses it into Samuel's hands as he leaves for work.

Weeks later, Samuel hands Nellie a wrinkled envelope. Nellie stares for a moment at the writing, so pretty and curved, in the center. She smoothes it out. Then she rips it open.

> dear Nellie,
> Letter from you arrived here. Happy!
> Letter from Mama not yet.
> Last I saw you, man in carriage took me.
> I stay at school. Cry.
> Teacher brought to me doll baby. Try feel better.
> I wait wait letter from Mama. I wait. I patient.
> Want soon I see sister Nellie.
> Biggest hugs,
> Bayla

Nellie reads and re-reads Bayla's letter, then tucks it into her skirt pocket. Soon, surely soon, Bayla will receive word from Mama and they will journey together to America! Nellie rushes to work now at the corset factory. All afternoon, she will feel the flat, folded letter upon her thigh as she sits at the sewing table, her fingers moving deftly, her head lost in thought about Bayla.

◆ ◆ ◆

It is dusk by the time Nellie looks up from the sewing table. She walks home quickly, breathing in the chilly, autumn air. As she passes by the park, she sees Sylvia walking toward her. Beside Sylvia is a young man, tall and handsome with black wavy hair. As he comes closer, Nellie can see that his chin has a small cleft in it, his eyes are round and dark like chestnuts. His hands make large, graceful strokes in the air.

"Hello. My name is Mordechai." His eyes dart to the ground, a sweet crinkle of a smile in his eyelids.

Nellie signs back: "I'm pleased to meet you." The three walk together in the direction of Lill's apartment, Nellie with a flush in her cheek and a thump in her chest.

◆ ◆ ◆

In a letter to Bayla, Nellie writes:

> *dear Bayla,*
> *Letter from you arrived. Excited!*
> *Big news, I meet man, deaf too. His name is Morde-chai.*
> *Walk everywhere together, happy!*
> *Dress now pretty, help me my friend Sylvia.*

— 197 —

Herschel cry Mama. Sad. I write letter again.
I wait and wait. Not patient. I miss my sister Bayla.
Biggest hugs!
Nellie

Months later, Nellie writes again.

dear Bayla,
Mordechai asked me marriage.
Cry happy!
Nothing, no letter from Mama.
You for me, please write letter to Mama.
Need must Mama Papa family come join us here.
Biggest hugs!
Nellie

Galicia 1886

PEARL STANDS AT THE SINK. *Little Sarah yanks at Pearl's skirts, but she hardly notices. How much time has passed since that carriage drove out of Tasse? Each week, each day, each minute her hope withers, and now Pearl persists—subsists— on the echo of a question: How can she reunite her family in America?*

Pearl receives letters from both Nellie and Bayla, cherished letters she reads over and over with quivering lips and pooling eyes. She takes out her own writing paper, she walks to the scribe. But then she turns back. Wordless. Mute. She cannot manage to reply.

One night, when Moshe comes home, Pearl begs him. Can they make a trip to Budapest at least, to check on Bayla? Moshe takes Pearl's face in his large, rough hands.

Three days later, they sit huddled in a carriage that clanks slowly through Budapest's uneven cobblestone streets. Pearl's stomach roils in tight knots. She rushes out of the carriage the moment it stops.

In the front office of the School, Pearl runs her finger along the careful scroll work of the oak secretary, inhales the distant scent of polish. From down the corridor, Bayla is walking toward her, the school administrator a step behind. Bayla has altered since leaving Tasse, Pearl thinks—her face is more angular; she is taller even. She is wearing an unfamiliar dress. Pearl pauses before her child, then she rushes toward her, pulling her in. Bayla is stiff at first, then melts into her mother.

Moshe shuffles into the office, speaks briefly to the administrator, then ushers Pearl and Bayla out through the heavy iron and glass doors into the chilled air. Pearl struggles to sign the few words she knew just a month ago. Down a narrow staircase, into a café, they sit together at a small round table. Moshe folds his hands in his lap, lowers his eyes. He knows no sign words at all.

Bayla looks at her parents expectantly. She is sure that they have come with news, that they have made plans, secured tickets, for the journey to America. She eats hungrily at first, then she slows, her eyes darting between her mother and her father.

"How are you, Bayla?" Pearl signs.

"All right, Mama. And you? I worried so, when you didn't write."

Pearl is lost, immediately, by Bayla's simple but fluid hand movements, by her own inability to answer back. She shoves her plate off to the side and leans in on crossed hands. Write? Pearl frowns. If Bayla only knew how many times she started a letter, only to tear it up in despair! Malkie, the Scribe—he thinks she is crazy. Maybe she is. But Pearl bears the weight of an ocean between Nellie and Bayla. Without good news, she cannot manage to post a letter.

Pearl searches Bayla's face. There is so much she wants to know: Is Bayla eating enough? She looks thin. Do the schoolmasters treat her kindly? Is she making friends there? But Pearl cannot ask, and she would not understand Bayla's answers even if she could. Pearl looks away from her daughter mournfully and slides her chair back a little. She gives Moshe a pleading look. Moshe proposes that they write out messages to Bayla—in Yiddish, just like Rayzl taught her. As Moshe walks off to ask the waiter for something to write on, Bayla signs to Pearl.

"Did you get letters from Nellie?"

Pearl nods her head, tears now streaking her cheeks. Bayla can't bear to bring up the news of Nellie's engagement. Instead, she takes a tattered piece of paper from her dress pocket. It has been folded and unfolded so many times, it nearly breaks into four squares as she delicately opens it. She holds it up for Pearl to see. A single hand form, drawn by Nellie: the sign word "soon."

Pearl's lips quiver into a smile, but Bayla can see how pained her mother is. She realizes now that her parents have not come with travel news, that there is no impending journey. With quaking hands, Bayla folds the paper along its creases and places it back into her pocket. She wants to beg, to plead with her mother and her father to get them to America! But the exhaustion in their faces, the weariness in their hunched shoulders, their fraying clothes, stops her. Bayla sits stiffly, her napkin tucked in her lap the way she learned in school, her back pressed flat against the upright café chair.

Pearl clasps Bayla's hand when they stand to leave, and they walk slowly down the street. When they reach the school office, Pearl hugs Bayla tight; Moshe caresses her cheek. Bayla steps away, and turns to walk down the corridor. She does not look back as her parents wave good-bye.

In her room, Bayla shakes; she can't stop shaking. She buries her head in her pillow and sobs. Beneath Bayla's dormitory window, Pearl falters as she steps into the carriage. She gasps for air as she sits on the hard bench, her own unheard cries lost in the shirt folds around Moshe's shoulder.

AT OUR KITCHEN TABLE, SOPHIA bent over a pad of paper and a basket of colored markers. It was a lazy Sunday morning, and while Bill and Juliet were out at the bagel shop, Sophia practiced writing her name in a rainbow array of colors, over and over again. Her letters were uneven and slanty, her S backward every time. I pulled a chair next to hers. Sophia gripped the thick pink marker to form a shaky, lopsided circle: a giant capital O.

Why hadn't I let Pearl write to Nellie and Bayla?

I stared out our huge kitchen window. Did I want to inject cruelness into Pearl? Amidst a painful separation, have her sever all contact, go wordless, leave her girls bereft of their mother, confused and despairing? Was I vindictive? I was jolted by Sophia posing a question while she worked away at her letters.

"Mama, why do me and Juliet have hearing loss, but you and Daddy don't?"

Ye Gods.

"Well, Soph," I ventured—collecting my thoughts while reminding myself that she was not yet five years old—"every baby gets a growing plan, half from its mother and half from its father. A growing plan has all sorts of commands, to help the baby develop and be healthy. One command is to get something called potassium to the baby's ears. In the growing plans Daddy and I passed to you, that command was missing. Daddy and I don't have hearing loss because when we were growing, each of our plans only had *half* of the missing command. But you and Juliet both got a *whole* missing command, half from each of us."

"So, will our babies be deaf?"

"Well, that will depend. Your babies will get their growing plans, half from you and half from their fathers. Your half will be missing the command. If the fathers' plans have the command, then your babies won't have hearing loss. If the fathers' plans are missing the command, then it's likely that your babies will be deaf. What do you think that would be like for you?"

After a long pause, "It would be ok. If we decided to, we could get our babies hearing aids or cochlear implants."

◆ ◆ ◆

While Sophia and I were talking, Bill and Juliet came home. Juliet settled herself on the kitchen floor beside us, her hands sticky with cream cheese, and set to work disabling her cochlear implant. She recently figured out how to reach to the back of her head and yank off the magnetic disc. She was one and a half now; her implant had been activated five months ago. It seemed she'd decided that hearing was hard work, and that she didn't always want sound. I placed the magnet on again, but she glowered at me and batted it back off. I didn't persist. I let her putter around the house soundlessly.

Juliet built a wooden tower, then knocked it down—without the kaboom. She typed on the keyboard of her play computer—without the click click click. I took her out to the swingset, and let her swing back and forth without the creak creak of the metal chains.

Juliet was happy enough for us to put her processor on each morning, but from then on, if a restaurant was too loud or she was tired, *yank*—and I rushed to catch her thousand dollar "ear" before she set it on a table smeared with ketchup or blue cheese dressing. Just as quickly, I raced to settle Juliet into a comfortable position, because with the blessing of quiet and the shut of her eyes, Juliet would fall asleep in seconds.

Juliet ripped her processor off at the sight of the blender

and the vacuum cleaner. She put it back on when she spied a favorite book we could read to her or a video she could watch. It was like a baseball cap—off for the bath, on for the playdate, off to skitter through the sprinkler, then back on for the cupcakes. I wondered sometimes whether to encourage it. Why *should* she hear the babies crying at the pediatrician's office if she doesn't have to? Why not miss the jackhammer blast when the car is stuck in traffic? Juliet sensed most of what was happening through vibrations anyway. Whether her sound was on or off, she knew when someone walked into the room, and she could read a face like a book.

Juliet's favorite face was Sophia's, and their play did not require hearing. Sophia put herself nose to nose with Juliet, locking eyes to secure her attention. Then Sophia led Juliet in play: they toted their baby dolls from room to room, they gave each other foot baths with bowls of warm water, they emptied every drawer in the house for inspection. They rigged up strings and cups and played telephone games. They put on music, whether or not they could hear it, and then they donned butterfly wings. So what if it was "Georgia Rae" that accompanied their dance moves and fairy games? So what if Bill and I might ourselves go deaf with the volume turned way up? They were having fun together, and they understood each other perfectly.

I marveled at the seeming irrelevance of sound. Juliet was fully ensconced in the life of our family and in the larger community all around her. She was bonding, exploring, playing, learning.

But not talking. Juliet was not talking yet. Juliet needed to hear in order to learn spoken language. With the lure of new storybooks, a set of bells, our old harmonica, we'd coax her and gently return the processing magnet—*glup*—to her head.

◆ ◆ ◆

Juliet was still waking up through the night. Like a jack-in-the-box, she'd pop up and yell at the top of her lungs. (*She didn't hear it!*) When I told my mother about Juliet's wake-ups, she suggested that Juliet might feel disconnected and scared without her sound, through the dark of night.

"You have no idea, Jenny, how disconnecting a hearing loss can be. I've struggled my whole life with disconnection," my mother said to me.

My mother's words, so plain and disclosing—they untied me. I asked her to tell me about her childhood ear infections, the surgeries, her hearing loss. I don't know why I had waited so long to ask her directly. My mother told me that she'd spent her childhood hiding her deafness. "Mouth

— 207 —

the words in chorus," my grandmother Mae had suggested, when my mother brought news of her second grade concert.

My mother got her first pair of hearing aids in her thirties when my oldest brother was born. She had struggled, lip-reading, before that.

"I wanted to be able to hear my children," my mother told me.

She went back to brainstorming about Juliet's sleep troubles, suggesting that, perhaps, Juliet could sleep with her implant processor on, or that Bill and I could talk to Juliet about her fears at night.

As my mother spoke, I imagined her sitting in an audiologist's chair, getting hearing aids for the first time. Maybe she held her new baby in her lap. Maybe she shivered as the cold silicon molded inside her ears. Her own mother, nowhere in sight.

My mother had wanted a string, a steady connection, to her children! It was her aim, her *longing*, no matter how tattered it turned out to be. It was *mine*.

She continued problem solving. We could try warm milk or chamomile tea at Juliet's bedtime, or calming music just before we removed her sound for the night. And as my mother spoke, I wondered at how my daughters' deafness had summoned her forward, steadied her, bridged her lost connections—enabling her to hear, and in hearing, to respond.

◆ ◆ ◆

One sunny morning in May, Juliet stood in the kitchen and signed for milk, her right hand pumping at an imaginary cow udder. Her hair was still a surprise of auburn—as unexpected as Bill's reddened beard stubble when he left off shaving—and it tumbled around her face, all waves and curls, like ribbon candy. Juliet was tinier even than Sophia was at that age, donning a pink and white sundress that billowed at her ankles. We would have been worried about her low weight, too, if we hadn't been through it before with Sophia. We could add all the butter and cream in the world. We simply made small children.

"You want milk?" I asked, signing to her as I spoke. "Sure," I continued narrating in my over-enunciating way, "I'll get you some."

I went to the fridge and took out the milk. As I poured milk into her bottle, I heard a word declared in a high, quiet register:

"Milk."

I turned on my heels, spilling milk all over the granite counter. Juliet's eyes danced and her cheeks rose with a slow, broad smile.

"Milk," she said again, now more loudly.

"Milk—yes!" I stuttered back in awe, and I grabbed her two hands and spun her long-armed around the kitchen, as she squealed with delight.

For the next few weeks, Bill and I danced through our days as we poured, drank and added MILK to everything! At the market, I stocked up: vanilla milk, coconut milk, condensed milk, buttermilk. Maple milk. Tiger's milk! Strawberry and chocolate milk. (Anyone for cocoa? So what if it's May?) Just to hear the precious utterance from Juliet's lips, again and again and again.

A flow of words came tumbling after: bye-bye, dog, yellow, top, shoe, ball, cup. Just like with Sophia, Juliet was hearing, and she was speaking! She sounded wonderful.

◆ ◆ ◆

Before Juliet started speaking, I was haunted by questions. Would the language center in Juliet's brain make sense of the electronic stimulations? Would she sound electronic? There was not a hint of Vader nor his friends in her voice. To hear Juliet speak just like a hearing child, with a clear, resonant voice, was amazing.

As Juliet's vocabulary grew, I kept a list of words on the fridge, as I had with Sophia. One day, I took down the girls' word lists and placed them side by side. At the stage when Sophia was seemingly obsessed with emotions—*happy, silly, angry*—Juliet was consumed with action verbs—*kick, run, throw*. Their distinctiveness—Sophia perching quietly in our arms, studying the faces around her; and Juliet rolling a ball, then jubilantly running to catch it—found expression even here, in the *order* of words that each child spoke.

◆ ◆ ◆

It wasn't long before Juliet was belting out "Tomorrow" from the musical *Annie*, in full voice, to anyone who would listen. After her "performances," she'd bend her body into a deep bow, her rosy cheeks soaking in the enthusiastic applause. Then Sophia would want a turn, and she'd take over with a ballad about white buffalo, or something from *The Sound of Music* or another musical we rented from the library.

Singing! Our girls were singing! Music was inside them, just as it was inside me, and they reveled in it. I began to warm up my voice, something I hadn't done for years, since the days when I had trained to sing opera. When I sang to Sophia and Juliet, they stilled and stared, studying my mouth, my face, in awed silence. Bill, too, showed his appreciation, chiding me for staying quiet for so long. In the car, we sang rounds of "Row, Row, Row Your Boat," until my voice cracked with the thrill of it, and I had to break off from my part, and take a catching breath, before starting up again.

At night, Bill and I removed the girls' sound systems, ran the bath, and placed Sophia and Juliet in the tub together. The transition from hearing to not hearing, as from clothed to unclothed, was seamless for them. Their play, and sometimes their arguing—"Juliet took my pinwheel, Mama! It really is mine"—went on uninterrupted. In the bath, they signed while they splashed, enjoying even the ill-given gift of water trumpets that made music they couldn't hear. Afterwards, goosebumps rubbed soft by warm towels, Sophia brushed Juliet's hair, moving gingerly around the implant scar, styling. Each time the brush caught the curls at the base of her neck, Juliet arched her head back and smiled, tickled by Sophia's gentle movements.

I watched them as they stood together on the dampened bath rug, laughing and shivering as their towels slipped down, and I wondered at all that we had given them and also stolen away. They came wired into this world able to bypass sound. It showed in their eyes, which stared things down until they understood them completely. And it showed in their peacefulness as they puttered about, damp hair pressed against their pajamas, gathering piles of books to look at before settling soundlessly into bed. We brought them access to sound, and with it worldly opportunities, but more selfishly, access to *our* experience and the form of language *we* use to express and describe it. I told myself that, when they were older, they could decide for themselves whether to hear and speak; they could take off their hearing technology if they preferred to, and live their lives Deaf. But deep down, I knew that was not entirely true. They were listeners now, understanding the world through audition; and they were speakers now, organizing their experiences into the categories of spoken language. We had placed them on one side of the divide. To straddle it looked impossible.

We didn't regret our decisions for Sophia and Juliet. But we feared the exclusions they might face. To some in the signing Deaf community, Sophia and Juliet would be outliers, hearing and speaking. They might even be offenders or traitors, having opted out of their deafness with technology and oral education. To some in the hearing world, Sophia and Juliet would be damaged, disabled, or at the very least, different. They had been taunted, already, by a hearing child: "You can't hear me, you can't hear me," a mean-spirited girl chanted while splashing in a kiddie pool one day. She had seen Sophia and Juliet hand Bill their hearing devices before they jumped into the water. Bill scolded the girl, and she seemed chastened, but afterwards, all I could think was how lucky Sophia and Juliet *were* to be unable to hear her. And how important it was for them to grow up strong, with confidence and self-esteem, and a sense of belonging.

Massachusetts, December 2006

SOPHIA AND JULIET HUDDLED in the window seat beneath our coziest fleece blanket. It was dark already, though it wasn't yet five o' clock. A short winter day. I'd tell stories until suppertime.

Lately, I had taken to revising old fairy tales. Rapunzel, high up in her tower, couldn't hear the prince so very well. When the prince yelled up, "Rapunzel, Rapunzel, let down your hair," Rapunzel rummaged among bartletts and boscs to hurl down a pear. Cinderella couldn't hear the clock strike midnight—the chime's frequency was too high—so in my version of the story, it was the sudden chafe of her old rags emerging beneath her sparkling gown that sent her running from the palace and into the woods. And Snow White missed entirely the knock on the seven dwarves' little arched door, and it was all for the best, because she never gave entry to the evil queen disguised as an old peddler woman with shiny, magic apples.

I was just taking up Rumpelstiltskin when the phone rang. I switched on a favorite book on tape—All of A Kind Family—and took the phone call. It was a mother I'd recently met. Her baby was deaf and she wanted recommendations of Sign Language books and Sign videos. When I hung up, the girls demanded to know who I was talking to, and what I was talking about. So I told them: "Do you remember the little baby, Lily? Well, Lily is deaf and her mom had some questions for me."

Sophia gave a nod of understanding and settled herself back into the cushions of the window seat to continue listening to the book. But Juliet stood looking at me.

"Lily's deaf?" she asked.

"Yes, honey."

"Deaf like Goya?" We had a children's video about the deaf painter, Goya.

"Yes. Deaf like Goya. And like you."

"*I'm* deaf?"

"Yes, Juliet, you're deaf."

"I'm *deaf*?"

"Yes, honey. You know how, when you take off your sound, you can't hear anything? That's because you're deaf."

"I'm *deaf*?"

"Uh—yes. You know how we play with Jan every week

at the Clarke School *for the Deaf,* and how all your friends there are deaf? You're deaf."

As I stood there, as incredulous as Juliet, I wondered suddenly, did I somehow forget to do or say something I was supposed to do or say? Had I omitted to inform Juliet of this basic fact of her life?

Our family's whole structure was framed around the fact of Sophia's and Juliet's deafness. Daily, we changed hearing aid and implant batteries like most parents changed diapers. We tested FM systems and cleaned earmolds. We scanned every restaurant, every room we walked into, for its acoustic qualities. And then there were all those recast fairy tales.

I tried to see it from Juliet's perspective. Each morning, like most little girls put on barrettes and headbands, she put on her implant processor. And with it, she was hearing. So she *wasn't* deaf. There was the little detail that she could turn her hearing off—she could remove her processor—and then she couldn't hear up to 112 decibels. She *was* deaf!

I knew that Juliet would one day recognize her deafness as a difference, and that her initial surprise at her deafness would, in all likelihood, morph—into loneliness when she couldn't hear the banter of classmates; into happiness when a true friend stopped to fill her in on what she missed; into fatigue when she met the muddle of relentless auditory input; into relief when she turned off her sound and recharged in a way unknown to hearing people.

Sophia was just starting to grapple with the ways her hearing loss might affect her life. One night, in the open span of our living room, Bill twirled Sophia while she held herself in long, graceful arabesque poses—a ballerina spinning around and around. Then, abruptly, she rearranged herself in Bill's arms, to be face to face with him.

"Daddy, do you think I'll dance like this at my wedding?"

"Yes, Sophia, I do."

"But"—she stammered—"do you think any one will love me—I mean, with my hearing aids?"

No hint of this before. *Her difference. And what it might mean.*

That night, as I tucked Sophia into bed, I said, "You know, Sophia, there are people in this world who make up reasons not to love others—because of the color of their skin, or their religion, or some other difference between them—but those people are not focused on what matters. If a person doesn't love you because you have a hearing loss, then that person is not worthy of your love. You are a wonderful person with a full heart, and those who know what matters in this life will come to know you and love you for who you are."

As I was saying all this, I wondered: is this really where I should be heading, into a discussion about social justice and prejudice? Shouldn't I just hug my girl and ask, with the disbelief I truly felt: "*You*—who can read any face, who can quiet any baby, who can cause any dog, however hyper, to settle calmly, magically, at your feet? *You*—whose eyes are rivaled only by Lake Tahoe's Emerald Bay? Someone not love *you*? Daddy and I are already buying bolts for the door to keep the hordes away."

But I didn't change my course. Sophia was telling us that she knew: she knew she had a difference. And she was asking us: would she be OK?

As we spoke, I thought of the prejudice, the pain, inflicted on Deaf people throughout history. Their "difference": a basis for denying them their intelligence, their humanity. I doubted that Nellie and Bayla escaped it.

Later, in a phone call to my sister, I wondered if I handled the conversation with Sophia very well. My sister assured me that it wouldn't be my last chance: I'd have all those teenage years to hone my response.

I dreaded to think of the teenage years; already both girls ripped off their sound when they didn't want to hear what we were saying. I'd read that it was typical of teenage deaf kids to take off their hearing technology to fit in at school. Not a winning strategy for academic success, or much else.

These days, Sophia wore her hair up in a high ponytail, seemingly proud of her new, fancy, gold-glitter earmolds. But I knew that one day her hair would come down to cover over, to camouflage, her hearing aids. I could only hope that the hiding impulse—so familiar, a pulsing in the vein—might be short-lived, and that she wouldn't remove her hearing aids altogether.

For now, Bill and I were all about staying positive. Deafness could mean colorful earware; funny fairy tale stories. So I got furious at my mother one day, during a visit to my parents' house. I was troubleshooting a problem with Juliet's earmold and implant processor when I overheard my mother say to Sophia,

"I just hate this. Don't you hate this?"

Sophia looked at my mother uncertainly, and said, "My earmolds aren't bothering me."

"No," my mother said, "Not the earmolds. The hearing loss. I hate it. Don't you hate it?"

At which point, I picked up Sophia and carried her into another room.

"Sophia," I said, as calmly as I could, "Grandma is frustrated because her hearing aids don't work very well. They whistle a lot—don't they?—and she has a lot of trouble hearing with them. Her earmolds bother her, too. They are made out of hard plastic, not like your soft ones, and they hurt her ears. That's why she was saying all that. She feels frustrated."

"Why doesn't Grandma get new hearing aids? Or put Vaseline on her earmolds, so they won't hurt so much."

"I'm not sure, honey. I'll suggest that."

Then I went to find my mother. Was it her own need for connection, for commiseration, that drove her, boundaryless, into such a leaky conversation with my daughter?

"What was *that* about?" I demanded. "Sophia is six years old, and she knows no other life. If she comes to hate her hearing loss, we'll deal with that. But let's not *lead* her there."

My mother apologized profusely.

New York, 1887

ON THE DAY BEFORE HER WEDDING, *Nellie does not bob in the center of a sea of friends, or dance through the streets wrapped tight in a flurry, a moving snowball of aunts or cousins, all figures in white. She does not bask in the calm of the one sister who knows her better than she knows herself. Nellie walks to the shul, to the woman's mikva bath for a ritual cleansing, alone.*

The following evening, just beyond the synagogue courtyard, Nellie stands shaking in her borrowed dress. A swish of tulle veils her freshly powdered face. Mordechai is already standing beneath the chuppah with his parents. The knots of his necktie and his shoelaces are undone in accordance with tradition, and he is wearing a white robe, a kittel. His hair is freshly cropped, his eyes bursting brown.

Nellie looks out at the small crowd: Elish and Herschel; Mordechai's brothers and sisters; Sylvia; Lill and Samuel Bau-

mann. They are all holding candles, yellow flames flickering before their eyes, their cheeks. Nellie draws a deep breath from her hollow stomach. Despite her letters pleading for her family to come, she stands without Bayla. Without Pearl.

Nellie shifts her weight. She feels hot in her dress. Her chest is tight and her mouth is dry from fasting. She worries, suddenly, that her breath is sour. Guests gather in close to recite blessings. Nellie fixes her eyes on Mordechai and lets the ceremonial wine settle her nerves. Mordechai slips a solid gold band onto her finger. His broad smile summons a flutter from deep in her belly.

Nellie does not hear the crunch of her petticoat, the shattering of glass beneath Mordechai's foot, the high whinny of the accordion. She lurches with Mordechai's passionate kiss on her lips. Before he leads her away from the guests, for a time of privacy, Lill clutches Nellie's face in her hands and kisses her forehead—an imprint, a jolt. Her mother, her father. Where on earth could they be? Still in Tasse? And where is Bayla—alone in a strange city—an airless dormitory room—in a scratchy school uniform? Nellie's heeled shoes sink into the sodden ground as Mordechai ushers her across the courtyard lawn.

◆ ◆ ◆

Weeks later Nellie stands in the kitchen, looking at the plants on the windowsill, puzzling over the strong smells in Mordechai's house. Did the herring spoil? Was the milk rancid? She walks downstairs and out onto the sidewalk, only to be assaulted by other overpowering smells: horse dung, the pungent scent of passing men, the burn of chestnuts from the pushcart on the corner. These days, Nellie can't get through market shopping without bringing along a flour sack stuffed with orange peels to hold to her nose. When the nausea hits, it accompanies her a full week before she realizes: she is pregnant. With Mordechai by her side as she lurches past the open pickle barrels, Nellie rejoices in her expectant condition.

By day, at work at the corset factory, Nellie dreams of her baby to come. By night, she dreams only of Tasse. She can't bear to write of the news to her sister, to her mother. To concede that they are nowhere near on their way. Nellie's belly grows round and taut; she puts her hand on her side, where she feels a flutter, a kick. Mordechai kisses her in that very spot, taps out a message of love with his hands. Then he kisses Nellie's cheeks, her forehead, her fluttering eyelids.

When the labor contractions start, Mordechai's mother sends for Lill and Sylvia, and together, the three women help Nellie birth her baby girl. By dawn, Nellie is holding her baby close, inhaling the warm dough of her cheek. She bounces her, spells B-E-R-T-H-A, an American name, with quick fingers along her baby's plump thigh. Her fingers move nonstop, full of doting and love, along her baby's tiny spine, across her diapered bottom, up the now-curling soles of her chubby feet.

It is Elish who first notices that Bertha does not blink her eyes or turn her head to sound. Even amidst the blasting of the shofar on Rosh Hoshana, when other babies cry, Bertha drifts in and out of sleep. One hundred blasts in all—single blasts at the call of Tekiah; a staccato series of three at the call of Shevarim; nine short blasts at the call of Teruah, and the longest mournful wail at the final call of Tekiah Godol—the New Year's calls to awaken, drift up to the ceiling unheard.

Elish comes to Nellie's room one night at bedtime. Nellie has a piece of string in her hands, and Elish watches as Nellie ties one end of the string around Bertha's tiny pink wrist. The other end, Nellie loops around her own wrist. Elish looks at her sister quizzically, and Nellie signs that the string tugs and wakes her when Bertha cries in the night.

"I think the baby is deaf," Elish signs.

"You do?"

"Yes."

"Why? Why do you think so?"

"She doesn't cry at loud noises; she doesn't even wake.

Watch." Elish claps her hands loudly behind Bertha's head. "Nothing. No. I am certain she doesn't hear."

Nellie stands over Bertha. With her unstrung hand, she wipes a droplet of milk from Bertha's face. Thoughts ricochet in Nellie's head, and her longing for Bayla surges stronger than ever. Elish taps Nellie on the arm, startling her. With eyes still fixed on her baby, Nellie signs, "It is good, Elish. It is good this way. Please, get Mordechai for me. He will want to know."

◆ ◆ ◆

On Friday afternoons, in the work-filled hours prior to the Sabbath, Nellie does not hear the scurried preparations. The chop-chop of onions, potatoes, and carrots. The squeak of the oven door. The whoosh of a hair brush. The soft rustle of silk.

Just before twilight, when the girls and women gather before the table, when Nellie stands with Bertha strapped to her chest—crisscrossed close and tied with Bayla's shawl—she does not hear the prayer over the candles, spoken and sung. She stands with Elish on one side, Mordechai's sisters on the other, and Nellie fights with her eyes. Opened, she sees her mother-in-law's lips moving in prayer. Closed . . .

When Nellie closes her eyes, she sees her past life. Pearl, circling her hands in the candlelight, her head covered with white lace. Moshe, striding home from shul, his eyes dancing with excitement, his bushy beard hiding away his words. Bayla, crouching in the nook beneath the windowsill, her signs sparking in the dusky shaft of a day's remaining light. All the little ones, crawling, toddling, running through the house. Rayzl, tumbling out of the carriage, her arms filled with tablets and chalk. Chava's belly jutting out from under her bedsheets.

As Nellie strives to make a house with Mordechai and his family, a deep pain burrows into the sockets of her eyes, and she fights to keep them from closing. She fights to rid her mind of its natural topics, to banish her internal questions about why she hasn't received word from her parents or Bayla, and why they haven't yet come. Her imagination strong-arms its way in: Bayla at school, Bayla alone amongst strangers on the High Holidays. Perhaps Bayla walked to the iron-girded bridge— Nellie saw it from the carriage—perhaps she walked there to throw hunks of bread into the rushing river beneath. To cast off the year's sins, to ask for and to grant forgiveness.

In Tasse, Nellie and Bayla played by the river while Pearl and Moshe and the other Jews of Tasse congregated at the water's edge, tossing crumbs, emptying their pockets, clutching hands, and embracing. Before Rayzl explained the Tashlich observance to them, Nellie and Bayla concocted their own explanations for why people tossed bread into the river on New

Year's Day—a winter's supply for the quick, gleaming fish or for the birds if they could get it; a procedure for thickening the river's mushy bottom, or for plumping the reeds. A day for cleaning—when else do the grown men stop to empty their pants pockets? The ritual made everyone's heart a bit lighter, whatever it was for, and Nellie and Bayla felt the gayness all around as people parted for their homes.

Now, staring off into the shine of the tea kettle, Nellie's trick eyes conjure Bayla, hunched over on a narrow school cot. Nellie does not know that Bayla has traveled by herself from Budapest to Hamburg, having borrowed money enough for a ticket to board the steamship Dania departing for New York. That she has slept on top of her bags in the ticket station for four nights, waiting for the ship to depart, eating only breads and cheeses. That she walked to a nearby market for provisions, not hearing the thief's footsteps behind her. That she reached her hand into her purse, then crumpled into an inconsolable ball, her face buried in her empty, open palms.

◆ ◆ ◆

Weeks later, Nellie receives a letter.

dear Nellie,

I tried to ride on boat Dania.

My money and boat ticket—thief grabbed. Gone.

Go back to school.

Teachers angry. Everyone angry.

Leave me by myself alone.

This letter for you I put in book, hidden. My friend
take book to library.

Want she finds letter and sends to you.

Wanted wanted I see my sister Nellie.

Now hope disappeared.

Galicia, 1888

IN TASSE, PEARL PACES BACK AND FORTH *across the kitchen floor, holding the Headmaster's letter. How could Bayla be so foolhardy? The dangers she might have faced—and now, an entire boatfare, lost!*

Pearl looks down at her cracked hands. It's her own fault! She should have written to Bayla. At the very least, she should have written to explain how they are trying—trying to save, trying to secure all the boat tickets. If Bayla knew this, she might not have struck out alone. What had Pearl been thinking? If tearing up her letters was self-punishment, it served to punish her children, too.

Nellie must be married a whole year already. Who knows? She may even be expecting a baby—the family's first grandchild. Without her. Without Bayla.

The saving is so slow, no matter how little they eat. Moshe is insistent now that they all travel together. But it will take years before they have enough money for so many boat tickets. One ticket with sponsors on both sides—that they can afford.

Pearl sifts through the papers on Moshe's desk. She finds several blank pages and carefully extracts them from the pile. She doesn't dare write on them herself. She folds them and sets them carefully at the bottom of her basket. Then she sets out to find Moshe, before walking once more to Malkie, the Scribe.

New York, 1888

BAYLA'S LETTER TO NELLIE is addressed, like the others, in care of Samuel Baumann. Samuel delivers this one himself, on his way to work. He does not let on to Nellie that he knows the news contained inside, that Pearl wrote to him already about the arrangements. He just stands by, a twinkle in his eyes, as Nellie opens the envelope and starts to read.

> dear Nellie,
> Mama bought ticket for me! Excited! Happy!
> Teacher lady ride carriage with me to boat.
> Samuel Baumann friend at New York harbor meet me.
> I get ready for long trip. Must practice voice name sound good!
> Must practice voice name sound perfect!
> I hug kiss my sister Nellie!
> I come! I come!

Massachusetts, August 2007

BILL BEGAN A NIGHTLY TRADITION of dancing with the girls after dinner. With his own (kid-friendly) rendition of Crazy Town's "Come my lady, Come, come my lady, You're my butterfly, Sugar, Baby," he'd lead Sophia and Juliet, dancing, to the playroom, or to the living room, or out onto the screened porch.

With the CD player loaded with "Sweet Baby James" and other favorites, Bill taught Sophia "the bump", and twirled her in the air in graceful ballet poses. Juliet combined chasing games and tumbling. I joined in, dancing with Bill, assisting Juliet in long arm flips, and pirouetting, hand in hand, with Sophia.

Yet in mid-song, nearly every night, I would break off— to throw the laundry in, to wipe down the table, to write in my journal. At some point in all the hoopla, the girls would come looking for me, charging at me, yelling exuberantly, "Mama, Mama," their arms wide open. They seemed to want to absorb me, to swallow me up. Sometimes, I felt the overwhelming urge to dodge them both, like a basketball player fake shooting to send blockers astray. I had work to do, and I wanted a bit of time to myself.

Their little faces were hopeful, their cheeks still curved with the chub that buoyed them in slow growth. They looked at me with their bright, sparkling eyes, as if I was the host of their treasure hunt. Their arms were wiry thin but strong; they heaved with the earnest determination to carry all that they could collect from me.

I stepped away, but they continued to follow me. I plied them with distractions—cinnamon sticks, acorn hats, a chocolate bunny. Anything. Take of anything. Just not of me.

But it was me that they wanted. As they sought to soak up every droplet, I wanted to yell out: *I am not as sweet and milky as I seem!*

I had stayed present through the crises. Despite my doubts and worries about mothering—despite my fear that disconnection was, in my family, an inheritable trait—I had forged steady connections with my daughters. I'd tended to them, I'd nourished them—and despite all the challenges, they were thriving and happy. They were hearing and talking. I could be proud of my mothering, proud of all that I'd overcome from within and from without to mother my girls well. Yet, more and more, as they grew sturdy and strong, I found myself withdrawing from them. Now that they were up and running—"on the air," as the audiologist liked to call it—I found myself receding. As I'd feared all along, I was turning inward. Away.

Just for a rest? I couldn't be sure.

Their deafness had jolted me into attentiveness. But now, it was no longer necessary for me to take notice of every sound around us, to reinforce every utterance they heard or made. I hoped it was a symptom of normalcy. After so much vigilance, I was finally just a tired mother, with the luxury to safely ignore my children.

Yet I feared it was otherwise. There was disconnection in my blood. It pumped through the generations. "Jenny, don't you hear Juliet? She's calling for you," Bill would say.

My attention was elsewhere.

Without intending it, I blocked out their chatter until they tugged on my sleeve. I didn't sit long with them. Restless, I excused myself to fold the towels rather than play. I ignored requests—Juliet would have to get her own sippy cup of water; Sophia could pull on her jumper by herself.

I couldn't construe my lack of attention as a strategy

for helping them become more independent. I was retreating. Even my writing projects—writing about them, writing about my longings to connect to them—served as an escape from being with them. I wanted to be separate, sometimes urgently, as if I'd vanish otherwise.

One afternoon, Juliet came to get me in my room. A babysitter was coming in a few minutes and I was dressing to meet Bill for dinner.

"What is it, honey?" I asked as I fiddled to get an earring on.

"Sophia hurt her back," Juliet said, and she waited for me to follow her to the playroom.

There I stood, a minute too long, fooling with the earring, jabbing my lobe persistently while Juliet waited, staring at me. And as I stood there, fiddling, not managing to get the earring into my pierced ear and not managing to move toward the playroom either, my eyes met Juliet's, reflected in the mirror, and I saw in my daughter's waiting gaze all that I knew and had known. At that moment, I gathered up my girl, apologizing, saying how silly of me, let's run down the stairs quickly. I felt lucky that, when we got there, Sophia was up and bouncing once again on our little trampoline.

Massachusetts, September 2007

THE NEXT FRIDAY NIGHT, I PREPARED to drive to my parents' house with the girls. My anger at my mother—at how she had spoken to Sophia about hating her hearing loss—had mostly subsided. Bill was traveling for work and the girls wanted to stay at my parents' house. My father would entertain them with the funny popping sound he could make by thrusting his finger into the inside pouch of his cheek. My mother would make their favorite fish dinner, let them carry around her bottles of shiny pink nail polish, and give them pretty ribbons and bows for their hair.

After packing up the car, I skittered with Sophia and Juliet, each hoisted in the crook of an arm, to the car. I buckled them into their car seats, handed them their blankets, then settled myself into the driver's seat, checking that I had my wallet and cell phone, water and snacks. Just before starting the engine, I twisted around to face them: "Want to take off your sound?" It was coming on nine o' clock, time for sleep.

Sophia gently dislodged her hearing aids. Juliet batted her hand at the wire of her cochlear implant processor, causing the magnetic disk to drop from her head.

I rifled through the CDs. I could listen to music on the drive. Anything I wanted, and as loud as I wanted, now that the girls didn't have their "sound." Maybe John Hiatt. He was always a favorite. "Georgia Rae" was playing by the time I turned on the highway. "Lucky for you, child, you look like your mama." I glanced in the rear view mirror. Both girls were sound asleep; cheeks flushed, hair matted like new seal pups. They did look like their mama, and I looked like mine.

Sophia woke up when I stopped the car in my parents' driveway. I left Juliet asleep in her seat while Sophia and I lugged in our stuff. The kitchen lights were bright enough for a police interrogation, and it smelled like roast turkey. There was a flurry of greetings and the usual question: "You left Juliet sleeping in the car?" I went back out to carry Juliet in through the other door where the lighting could be dimmed.

Back in the kitchen, my parents had returned to whatever they were doing before we arrived. Sophia was drawing a picture—all hearts and flowers—with colored markers. When she finished, I carried her off to bed, hoping the picture she made would remain on the refrigerator where I mounted it, and not be folded into the big wicker trash barrel.

I woke the next morning to the sound of my father's violin. The girls were out of bed already, and I found them sitting on the couch, intently listening to my father practicing a Beethoven sonata. When they saw me, they begged to take a bath in my mother's newly remodeled bathroom. The bathtub was a swimming pool for them, with jet bubbles and new toys. "Sure," I said, and I went to fill up the tub.

Warm water rushed into the tub as Sophia and Juliet gleefully yanked off their pajamas. Hearing devices were piled high, whistling and blinking, into my one dry palm, as my girls slipped into the bubbling water together and instantly, wordlessly, began a game of handing each other "fountain drink" supplies—tall plastic cups to fill with water then "top off" with bath foam to create hot chocolate with whipped cream.

Watching Sophia and Juliet, their eyes locked now in soundless communion, I thought of Nellie and Bayla. Reunited, at last, in America. Walking briskly together down Union Street in Brooklyn, their hands soaring, alive with their old home signs, until their arms linked and they shared the silence of all but the pulse reverberating in the crook of their interlocked elbows. I never did find a Census Report or any other document showing Bayla arriving in America. But she *had* to have come. Across an ocean, to a new world. She had to. To lock elbows with her sister.

In the bath, Juliet had just learned how to lean backward in the water to wet her hair, and now she wanted the shampoo. I squeezed some strawberry-scented shampoo in her palm and she rubbed it on her temples. Then she abruptly stood up, lather streaking down the sides of her face, her belly and legs. She scrambled out of the tub, refusing to allow me to rinse the shampoo out of her hair. I scooped her up, wrapped her in a fluffy towel, and tried to hold her over the tub while pouring cupfuls of water on her hair. Sophia was busy crafting beards and goatees on her chin with the excess bubbles in the bath.

My mother came in and offered to help rinse Juliet's hair. Juliet was yelling in protest, and I struggled to keep hold of her and the oversized towel she was now only half-wrapped in. My mother went to her cabinet and quickly returned with two cottonballs. She gently lodged one in each of Juliet's ears. "She may not like the feeling of water in her ears," is all she said. I looked into my mother's face and smiled out a "thank you."

Juliet relaxed, or resigned herself, and I cradled her over the bathtub as my mother rinsed Juliet's hair, careful not to get any water in her eyes or ears. The soft flow of warm strawberry-scented water gently rippled and ran from Juliet's silky hair.

"You are a wonderful mother," my mother said to me, her eyes fixed on the run of water. "I'm so relieved, Jenny. Relieved that you can mother your children in a way I wasn't able to mother you." As I watched my mother guide the stream of water over Juliet's hair, I could almost feel the water trickle at my own temple, the quick soak of the cotton ball chilly along the rim of my ear.

When my mother's eyes met mine, they were the softest, palest shade of sea.

◆ ◆ ◆

Later that night, at bedtime, I looked on as Juliet put her favorite pink pony to sleep. She nestled the pony's head on her pillow, then picked up a book. But rather than pretend-read it to the pony, Juliet began to rustle the book's pages loudly, just by the pony's ear. To me, she said simply, "My pony likes hearing for sleep."

I spoke to Juliet about her sleep problems, as my mother had suggested a while back.

"Juliet, would you want to try sleeping with your sound? Grandma thought you might want to. You can leave your processor on, you know. Then you can hear all the sounds of the house while you're sleeping."

Juliet nodded her head.

I settled Juliet into bed, with her processor on. But within a few minutes, she yanked it off. "No—I don't want my sound," she said. She wasn't used to sleeping with sound; or maybe she preferred the quiet. I braced myself for the repeat awakenings, hoping that Bill at least would get a good night's sleep in his hotel, after work.

As I lay in bed that night, I thought about my mother and me: how we were both climbing a steep learning curve, straining to listen. How it was deafness that brought us here. My daughters' deafness. My ancestors'. My mother's. My own. How we were reaching out. An embrace by the river's edge, pockets empty.

I felt full of forgiveness then, toward my mother and toward myself. I *was* mothering my children whole, in spite of my holes, my impediments. The impulse to tune out—familiar to all parents, yet more concerning to me given my history—would not rule me. I could combat deafness in myself as much as in my girls; I was sure of it. For the first time in my parents' house, I was moored. Sophia and Juliet were breathing softly, sound asleep in the bed beside me. Teaching me.

◆ ◆ ◆

Sometimes I stared at my hands, my arms—I had located my historical inheritance there, somehow—in the run of veins that bulged close to the surface of my skin, crisscrossing thick and blue. At birth, my blood had to be transfused four times. Whose blood went in, whose out? My father's? My mother's? My mother's blood was RH negative, not to be lent again. But I was certain: what pulsed in my veins was undeniably hers. And what pulsed in hers, the inheritance of the ages. A swelling emptiness, a deafness to fight against. I would fight to hear my girls.

Back home on a Monday afternoon, Juliet was talking to Sophia, telling her about her first day at the Clarke School preschool program. Sophia was to start her new school the next day.

"Sophia, we're gonna have caterpillars and butterflies at school. It's really true. And Miss Heather gave me a snack. And I rided the bus!"

I heard Sophia gently correct Juliet:

"You're supposed to say I *rode* the bus. C'mon, Juliet, let's play in the fort."

With a running start from the front hallway, Sophia and Juliet hurtled over the couch and landed in a sea of pillows walled in by tall cushions.

The veins in my hand throbbed and my wrist flicked as I thought of strings tugging in the night. In deafness, my ancestors found a way to hear their babies. And they gave to their babies a way to be heard.

Sophia and Juliet were flourishing, and my fears for them receded daily, as Sophia spoke to friends on the phone, as Juliet took to whispering secrets in Bill's ear. They were full of make-believe and surprises. Like natural wordsmiths, they concocted stories more imaginative than anything I could conjure up. Bailey, the goat, jumped high in the sky and floated motionlessly among the clouds to escape a monster's notice; then, after a tasty lunch of cloud fruit, was led home by a baby "leader" owl, just hatched at the edge of the sea. They drew illustrations, invented sequels. They dialed my mother to share their tales, all parties using maximum volume telephone speakers.

I was frayed and tattered. Fatigued—but not unraveled.

My voice, like their voices, emerging. My ears, theirs.

We would hear each other.

And we would listen.

I jumped into the fort, to be with my girls.

Acknowledgments

THE STORY I HAVE WRITTEN has more to do with emotional memory and imagination than with history. In writing about the people I love, I have inevitably rewritten them to fit with my own perception of truth. As Mark Doty says, "distortion is the betrayal built into memoir, into the telling of memories." The story I have written is singly my own.

Thank you to Marilyn Abildskov, my mentor, for perceiving the light of my story and for nurturing me until I could see it myself. Thank you to Rebecca Gradinger, my agent, for recognizing the emotional heart of my work, and for always encouraging me to return to my writing table. Thank you to Gloria Jacobs, my editor—full of wisdom, grace, and warmth—and to everyone at the Feminist Press who brought their expertise and enthusiasm to the production of this book.

Gideon Yaffe read an early draft by headlamp at 2 a.m. the first night of a visit, and spent the subsequent days in thoughtful conversation with me as our kids rode endlessly on carousels. Becky Michaels read and *re*-read this book, and with her quiet brilliance found solutions to problems over which I'd still be scratching my head today. Diana Larkin and Missy Wick gave me countless hours of advice and lent me Northampton writing homes full of warmth and encouragement. Sarah Buss got me to Iowa City—my favorite of all writing places—and spoiled me every free minute I was there.

For years, I have sat, inspired, beside dear and extraordinary writers at workshops led by Robin Barber, Carol Edelstein, Linda McCullough Moore, and the MEOWS. Many wonderful friends have brought me wisdom about writing and parenting: Claudia Canale-Parola, Tracy Smith-Camenisch, T. Susie Chang, Barbara Considine, Nancy Garlock, Chaia Heller, Ann Hulley, Amy Kroin, Susan Leeds, Meredith Michaels, Julia Mintz, Robert Radin, Elaine Stinson, Stephanie Vargas, and Lynn Yanis.

Valerie Stanik, Phyllis Shushan, and Andrea Olkin helped me with family geneology. Liz Rosenberg supplied an eleventh-hour translation. Sarah Burkman, Liana Doyle, Lon Otto, and Sandra Scofield commented with discernment on earlier drafts. Marc Neisen helped me to unlock memories, and Lula Mae Asberry jumped at every opportunity to reminisce.

Sara Just and Keith Lucas have stood by me since the beginning. Cathy Bendor, the Karpels, Jennine Kirby, Lisa McLeod, the Millner/Newmans, Vance Ricks, Matthew Tarran, and Susan Verducci—ever true and lasting.

Janice Gatty brought Sophia and Juliet into the speaking world. Jean Ferris and Kathie Betts opened up all avenues of communication. Peter Kenny, Marilyn Neault, and Dennis Poe ministered to our every medical need. I can never repay them.

Becoming a parent has deepened my love and respect for my mother and father. Watching my daughters grow in their relationship with one another has strengthened my connection to my sister and my brothers. This book reveals a loneliness, a deafness I experienced within my family as a child. It is with open ears that I find myself received by them now.

My husband, Bill, with a tender, steady, and perceiving love, has journeyed with me on a circuitous path of loss to a wholeness we could have hardly imagined. I dedicate this book to him and to our daughters, Sophia and Juliet, who inspire me, improve me, and fill me, minute to minute, with joy and wonder.

The Feminist Press is an independent nonprofit literary publisher that promotes freedom of expression and social justice. We publish exciting writing by women and men who share an activist spirit and a belief in choice and equality. Founded in 1970, we began by rescuing "lost" works by writers such as Zora Neale Hurston and Charlotte Perkins Gilman, and established our publishing program with books by American writers of diverse racial and class backgrounds. Since then we have also been bringing works from around the world to North American readers. We seek out innovative, often surprising books that tell a different story.

See our complete list of books on at **feministpress.org**, and join the Friends of FP to receive all our books at a great discount.

THE FEMINIST PRESS
AT THE CITY UNIVERSITY OF NEW YORK
FEMINISTPRESS.ORG